"An indispensable guide for sellers who want to make the 'impossible' sale. After reading this book, you'll have no excuse not to play big."

—JILL KONRATH, author, *Agile Selling*

"With intriguing stories and sound advice, *Scrappy* provides the recipe book for building a business with original, unexpected ingredients."

—JAY BAER, author, *Hug Your Haters*

"As a healthcare leader, working in an industry that is experiencing dramatic and unrelenting change more than any time since the 1960s, with increasing government regulations and never-ending cost pressures, [I know that] our industry must accelerate its transformation and needs more people who are willing to get 'scrappy.' Thinking big, taking risk, and [having] the willingness to be 'all in' on new, transformative ideas are what healthcare needs, and Sjodin's book is a great resource to help us get there. Through engaging real-life stories, along with a practical, easy-to-follow framework, this book will increase the likelihood of success in your career and may inspire you to experience something new and different in your personal life as well.

No matter your profession, reading this thought-provoking book will provide you with a competitive advantage. The principles you will learn can be applied to any goal, making *Scrappy* a must read for anyone looking to set themselves apart and achieve new heights."

—RAY CHICOINE, president, Monarch HealthCare

"Throughout the book, I was thinking about the kids Olive Crest serves and realized a lot of them need to be scrappy in order to get out of their situations. Wouldn't it be awesome someday to incorporate this training for our kids especially going into adulthood? . . . This book is clever, with practical ideas that can help people in their careers, in dealing with their families, and in navigating the world around them."

—DONALD VERLEUR, CEO, Olive Crest

"Whether you are a CEO of a Fortune 500 company looking to jump-start your organization, mid career and contemplating your next move, or a recent college grad scrambling for your big break, Terri Sjodin's *Scrappy* has smart

advice. It's not the typical 'rags to riches' stories of celebrities, but rather a set of experiences from people we can all relate to. Great content and a fun, quick read. Can't beat that!"   **—TIMOTHY PUNKE,**
senior vice president, Weyerhaeuser

"There are many times when I found myself smiling or laughing out loud. *Scrappy* is engaging, entertaining, and inspiring. I love so many things about this book."   **—COURTNEY NOELLE MADDOX,**
president of sales and marketing and cofounder, Girl ExtraOrdinaire

"Terri shows how being scrappy really works and how readers can implement concrete techniques into their personal and professional lives. We will use the book as a staple for our sales training. But more important, I will study it with my young-adult children to help them become successful in life."
—HOWARD E. SHARFMAN,
senior managing director, NFP Insurance Solutions

"Terri delivers a tremendous real-world guide on how to awaken the scrappy spirit within you. This little book is big on practical ideas and will save you a ton of time."   **—DAVE MCLURG,**
chairman, The Board International™

"If you have a thirst for more success, *Scrappy* is your secret sauce."
—TODD DUNCAN, CEO and founder,
The Todd Duncan Group LLC; author, *High Trust Selling*

"A fast, easy read with real-world insight that actually teaches you how to be 'scrappy' and win. This book gives personal and professional insight on why staying scrappy gets you the biggest reward. Each chapter inspires as it challenges you to take action."   **—TERRY WATSON, VICE PRESIDENT,**
Channel Marketing, Hubbell Power Systems, Inc.

"This book will show readers how they can take their personal and professional lives to the next level with a simple shift in their approach to life."
—SHERYL O'LOUGHLIN, CEO, REBBL Inc.;
former CEO, Clif Bar & Company; cofounder, Plum Organics

SCRAPPY

ALSO BY TERRI L. SJODIN

Small Message, Big Impact:
The Elevator Speech Effect

New Sales Speak:
The 9 Biggest Sales Presentation Mistakes
and How to Avoid Them

SCRAPPY

A Little Book About Choosing to Play Big

Terri L. Sjodin

Portfolio / Penguin

An imprint of Penguin Random House LLC
375 Hudson Street
New York, New York 10014
penguin.com

Illustrations on pages 7, 21, 60, 145, 184, and 213 courtesy of Mitt Seely
Image on page 84 © Brandon Steiner

LIBRARY OF CONGRESS CATALOGING-IN-PUBLICATION DATA
Names: Sjodin, Terri L., author.
Title: Scrappy : a little book about choosing to play big / Terri L. Sjodin.
Description: New York : Portfolio/Penguin, [2016]
Identifiers: LCCN 2016017406 | ISBN 9781591848356 (print) |
    ISBN 9780698411821 (ebook)
Subjects: LCSH: Success in business. | Attitude (Psychology) | Strategic planning.
Classification: LCC HF5386 .S62185 2016 | DDC 658.4/09—dc23 LC record available
    at https://lccn.loc.gov/2016017406

Printed in the United States of America
10 9 8 7 6 5 4 3 2

This book is dedicated to all my scrappy girlfriends who are
"full of fighting spirit" and know how to "kick a little ass."
My BFFs Nicole, Pattie, Joey, and of course all the girls in my pack:

Contents

CONTENTS

SCRAPPY

INTRODUCTION

WHILE I CAN'T PINPOINT THE FIRST TIME I HEARD THE WORD "scrappy," I do recall becoming aware of the idea, the feeling of it, the notion of *doing something* to stand out from other people going after the same opportunities I wanted. Here's the backstory: It was 1988, and I had just graduated from college and was beginning to launch my career. Differentiating myself from other hopeful, prepared, hardworking candidates with solid résumés was something I knew was vitally important for my success. The challenge was that I didn't have contacts, a network, or an Ivy League degree to gain access to the people who could help me, and it seemed as though I was getting screened out of prospective jobs before getting a shot. That feeling was frustrating and discouraging. I felt there had to be a better way.

The advice I heard most often was to "be patient," and that if I paid my dues and kept "working at it," I would gain enough experience through the "school of hard knocks" to learn how to "get the job done." That was exactly the opposite of what I wanted to hear. I was determined to get there faster, smarter, and with class and style.

Not knowing how to make that happen, I was looking for clues. Then one ordinary Friday night at the movies with friends, everything shifted. We were watching the Oliver Stone film *Wall Street*, and a specific sequence of scenes provided just what I needed: It changed my perspective and opened the door to this notion of getting "scrappy."

Bud Fox, an ambitious young stockbroker portrayed by Charlie Sheen, was trying to build his portfolio of clients, and Gordon Gekko, a powerful corporate raider played by Michael Douglas, was a "dream prospect" but also a seemingly impossible person to reach. To get a shot, Bud decided to do something to stand out from his competitors. He called Gordon Gekko's office every day for fifty-nine days in a row and crafted a plan to visit Gekko on his birthday to present him with a box of his favorite type of rare cigars. Gekko was impressed with Bud's daring effort and granted him an interview. It was creative, a little costly, bold, and scrappy. It earned Bud Fox a few minutes with the key decision maker he'd been seeking.

The whole plan—the homework, the cigars, and the effort to bond with Gordon Gekko's assistant—got Bud Fox in the door. He got his shot, and I got the lesson.

Over the years, I have gone back to this scrappy moment as motivation to get past a challenge, and it still works for me. My snapshot reference to *Wall Street* is not about the archetypal portrayal of 1980s excess—it was merely the trigger that set in motion my own efforts to be a "scrapper" and get scrappy for the first time. Bud Fox was the example I needed, and the film inspired me to take some definitive action—so I did. I'll share some of these stories with you later in the book.

Now, more than twenty-five years later, nothing has really changed. Sure, the landscape is different, and I have more contacts, but I still get scrappy to break through barriers, meet challenges, and find solutions. It is a vital piece of every professional challenge I face. Sometimes I have to employ a detailed strategy or plan to connect with the right people to get where I want to go. Other times developing a plan isn't possible and I simply have to "punt." Ultimately, I have developed a checklist of sorts, allowing for flexibility in various circumstances.

WHY GETTING SCRAPPY MATTERS

We all have dreams, wishes, and hopes for the future—a desire to accomplish certain things in our lives. We all experience challenging situations that make us say, "Okay, now what?" We hope someday we will get a break and it will magically happen (whatever your "it" is, right?). As time goes by, we may find ourselves so deeply entrenched in daily life that our dreams can get pushed aside. We realize they don't come easily. Sometimes, even when we do get a shot at a dream, it feels like the odds are stacked against us. The competition is tough and we know it! So sometimes we postpone our efforts—or maybe even self-select out.

Maybe you're standing at a crossroads or have encountered a

roadblock. Maybe you just aren't sure what's next. This book is the result of my feeling that way too. Under these same circumstances, when I'm stuck, I look to those inspiring individuals who have what I call a "scrappy mindset"—or "scrappers."

A scrapper is a person who is a fighter or serious competitor, especially one always ready or eager for a bout or contest. Think in terms of the best lightweight scrapper in boxing. Let's not take this literally—you don't need to be overly aggressive and get in a scuffle. I'm speaking to the spirit of the word. To simply call their scrappy successes miracles or lucky breaks would suggest it is not possible to replicate their methods, but the good news is you can. Scrappers don't just think about what could be—they execute a scrappy effort and make things happen.

Through the years, I have followed their lead and attempted to break through barriers, find a window when I can't go through the front door, and beat the odds. Sometimes it works, sometimes it doesn't. But it always feels better to do something and shake things up a bit. Even when a plan fails to work, it creates new avenues of thought and other pathways that push things forward.

Even if the chances of being seen, heard, discovered, or selected for a specific opportunity seem slim, when you get the chance, how do you make it count? How do you make yourself stand out? How do you get noticed in a positive way? Simple. You apply resourceful and creative inspiration to your situation and give yourself the edge. You work smarter and get scrappy!

Anyone can be scrappy. It's a choice to play big, or at least big for you. It's what you do when you're all in and ready to put your tush on the line.

THE IMPETUS OF THIS BOOK

This concept of getting scrappy has not only been part of my personal business strategy, it's also been a key piece of my work as a presentation skills consultant. Why? Because what good is a solid presentation if you can't get in the door to deliver your message to the right person? There's no easy access to the most desirable listeners or decision makers. We are not entitled to a person's time and attention. More often than not, we must earn the right to be heard. I dedicated an entire chapter to this idea in my previous book, *Small Message, Big Impact*. This book is simply a practical and—I hope—inspiring companion to those thoughts.

Since writing *Small Message, Big Impact*, I have received calls and e-mails from scores of people who want and need scrappy ideas and suggestions. They're ready to play bigger and they have questions about how to get started and how to craft a winning effort.

Those inquiries prompted me to explore the idea further, conduct some research, and identify a pattern that could be shared and duplicated. I interviewed individuals whose success was significantly impacted by their scrappy efforts. Their stories are inspiring and thought provoking.

This information has now been compiled into an easy-to-access format with tools designed to help you jump-start your next scrappy effort and reach your goals easier and faster.

This is not another book about persistence, although scrappy and persistent are a winning combination. Persistence is certainly a factor, at times. Initiative is a factor. Heart and passion are factors. But the scrappy piece of the puzzle is also about getting tactical in a specific way, at the precise moment you need to. One thing is for sure—nothing pisses off the persistent person more than the scrappy person who steps in and pulls off a classy, amazing effort and gets the deal, the win, or the opportunity. In today's competitive market it takes more than just creativity, more than just persistence, more than just a dream. Sometimes you have to get scrappy to make things happen.

WHAT YOU WILL LEARN

Join me as we explore this idea of getting scrappy—what it is, what it isn't, and how people from all walks of life have employed the art and science of scrappiness to develop tactical approaches that changed the game for them and moved them closer to their goals.

Getting scrappy relates to attitude, strategy, and execution. We will explore each of these three areas in the chapters ahead.

You Will Learn:

- Why getting scrappy is a choice to play big
- Why deciding "to go" is the first step
- The components necessary to develop a scrappy approach
- How to cultivate your best ideas
- How to manage risk and bounce back from mistakes and failure
- How to scale a scrappy culture and strategy within an organization
- The value of leaving room for serendipity
- How to execute your plan when you're ready to put your tush on the line

What I know for sure is that your scrappy mindset will evolve over time. For some of you who already relate to the idea of getting scrappy, this book will help you take your efforts to an entirely new level. If this is a new or foreign concept for you, don't worry. You're not alone. Most people have not been encouraged to get scrappy. Getting scrappy isn't a topic taught in academic environments or even in a traditional workplace. Quite the opposite.

That's why it works. It's practical and tactical, and the results will be transformational.

I have discovered that this material is as much about living your personal life adventure as it is about marketing and achieving goals. We are the main characters of our own life story, and when you get scrappy, it makes for fun and interesting chapters.

As we move forward, have a little fun! This book is for people who are ready to change their circumstances and shake up the status quo. Soon you can begin crafting a strategy and executing a plan that works well for you. It doesn't have to be perfect to work. What's important is that you get to be *you* while still playing the game. You have the opportunity right now to awaken the scrappy spirit within you and shift your future to an entirely different place. Different parts of this book will appeal to you at various times in life and for a host of reasons. So stay open and curious about the possibilities ahead.

Get in the ring and play big!

Chapter 1

WHY GET SCRAPPY

BACK IN THE MID 1970S, I WAS A GIRL SCOUT. PART OF THE adventure of scouting was participating in the annual Girl Scout cookie drive. In addition to receiving awards for selling a certain number of boxes, we could earn money toward paying for camp and raise funds for our troop.

In case you think selling Girl Scout cookies is easy, let me assure you—it is not. Back in my day, you canvassed your neighborhood, walking door-to-door, with an order form in hand to encourage folks to indulge in their favorite cookies. After taking the orders, you waited weeks for the cookies to arrive, and when they did, you had to sort and organize them and then walk door-to-door *again*, delivering all of the boxes and collecting the money so you could turn it in to the troop leader. It didn't always go smoothly, and there were often many challenges along the way. Sometimes people wouldn't be home. Sometimes if they were home, they didn't have the money so you had to go back another time. Sometimes people changed their minds and didn't want their cookies. Others wanted more cookies, and then you would need to order more inventory and start the process all over again. The big goal was to sell a hundred boxes, and I was persistent, but it was no easy feat.

Fast-forward to 2014. Imagine my delight when I read an article in the *Los Angeles Times* with the headline "GIRL SCOUT SELLS COOKIES OUTSIDE POT DISPENSARY: 117 BOXES IN 2 HOURS." I thought to myself, "Brilliant!"

Danielle Lei, a thirteen-year-old Girl Scout, and her mom, Carol, took an entirely creative approach to the annual sale of Thin Mints, Samoas, and Tagalongs. Lei simply blew the curve by forgoing the traditional sales approach and focused on a specific market with a proven fondness for . . . cookies. She sold more than a hundred boxes in two hours and at the forty-five-minute mark she had to replenish her supplies. It wasn't magic or luck. Lei and her mom sized up their obstacle—selling a large amount of Girl Scout cookies in a flooded market—and stepped into a space of creative and inspired thought—placing their stand outside a pot shop.

In addition, she eliminated the biggest challenges with her scrappy approach: no door-to-door selling or delivery. Her table of cookies made it easy to manage the requests of people wanting more cookies on the spot, and it eliminated wasted time, energy, and effort.

Damn! That was scrappy!

My old-school strategy showed my persistence and might still work, but quite frankly, Danielle's was better. Selling 117 boxes in two hours? That's outstanding. Her scrappy strategy beat my persistence, that's for sure.

One of the reasons I enjoy Danielle Lei's Girl Scout cookies story is that it was a pleasant surprise, an amusing departure from the norm. Those are the scrappy efforts people remember, talk about, promote, and support. On an average day, when nothing out of the ordinary happens, and someone does something special that makes you smile or brightens your day, it is welcomed and appreciated. There's nothing better than a pleasant surprise, no matter how big or small. When someone executes a plan that's clever, we notice! In Danielle's case, a simple no-cost effort made national news, and lots of people were talking about her idea. Every time I share this story, I hear, "Wow, that was clever! Of course she sold a ton of cookies." (While I imagine the official Girl Scouts position does not encourage young ladies to replicate her effort, I think you get the point.)

SCRAPPY DEFINED

So why the word "scrappy"? Why that adjective? Scrappy can be defined as "full of fighting spirit." It is synonymous with having moxie, being feisty, enthusiastic, gutsy, lively, and spunky. The *Urban Dictionary* puts it a little more bluntly: "A person who is little but can really kick some ass." I like that one too. The word "scrappy" embodies the mix of all these traits, plus the gumption to take action!

To be scrappy is to have the determination of a street fighter, to work smarter, to be willing to work harder when you need to, to take risks and play big no matter what the obstacles or opposition.

The notion of "getting scrappy" is bound up in the effort to get around an obstacle or challenge faster, smarter—in a clever way, even "against the odds." Scrappiness is not just about doing something difficult, though at times that's part of it. Getting scrappy is also about getting something done despite opposition. It's about the platoon outflanking an army, David slaying Goliath with a slingshot, punching above your weight. Don't get me wrong. Big guys and gals can be scrappy. Big companies can be scrappy—but in order to succeed, a scrappy mindset is necessary. Complacency isn't scrappy. Mediocrity isn't scrappy.

ON PLAYING BIG

The tales of people who pull off the seemingly impossible wins or who have achieved crazy fun goals inspire and challenge us to believe in our own dreams of playing a little bigger. We hear about their successes (and big painful losses, which also make good stories) and tend to focus on the end result, but what are we missing here?

I think it's the details, the thoughts, and the way these individuals creatively navigated the challenges along the way that we can learn from. There are things that happen, choices they make at the turning points, speed bumps, and roadblocks in their path that change the game. There's something that happens the moment you truly decide *to play big* that makes the difference. Just when it seems like their story is over—but it's not, and then it is, and then it's not—they try another way, and we say, "I can't believe they did that. Damn, that was scrappy!"

When it comes to playing big, a scrapper doesn't do anything that is illegal, unethical, or immoral. My motto is "Let's keep it classy and scrappy." I truly believe in the value of creating a positive disruption. Having said that, there are times when good ideas have gone bad, and we'll discuss those too.

KNOWING WHEN TO GET SCRAPPY

A scrappy effort might begin when you have a specific goal with a specific challenge to circumvent, most likely within a limited time frame. Or maybe you have hit a wall, gotten stuck, need a change, or just simply want more. Sometimes people say, "Well, I'm fine. Things could always be worse." That's when I immediately think of my friend Pam Jett, who once said to me, "Just because things could be worse doesn't mean you don't deserve better." Truth is truth.

Of course we've all heard the countless examples of legendary scrappy stories about now-famous entrepreneurs such as Steve Jobs, Mark Zuckerberg, and Oprah Winfrey. But there are even more everyday, nonfamous people, from Girl Scouts to start-up entrepreneurs and high-level executives, pulling off incredibly scrappy feats—small, medium, and large—on a regular basis. We can gain some practical, tactical ideas from these individuals.

Maybe it's down to you and three other candidates for a job. All things being equal, how are you going to distinguish yourself from your competition? Perhaps you need capital for your dream venture. Maybe you need to close a deal to keep your company afloat. Maybe you just need access to a particularly hard-to-reach decision maker. Whatever goal you have set for yourself, at this point maybe it's time to make some small but powerful changes in your approach to executing a more proactive strategy in these types of situations.

The exceptional life depends not on working harder, but on "different," even opposite actions from habit and the crowd.

—Ralph Waldo Emerson

HOW GETTING SCRAPPY CAN HELP YOU

Consider all the different ways you can engage in a scrappy effort to change or improve your circumstances or start down the path toward a future goal. Here's a quick snapshot of the wide variety of benefits getting scrappy can produce. It can help you to:

- Earn the right to be heard
- Gain access to a person who can help you
- Share an idea
- Rebound after any disappointment
- Get out of "purgatory" after getting no response at all
- Get access to a financial investor
- Secure a distribution partner for your product or service
- Land a job
- Be promoted
- Close a deal
- Get the best mentor
- Get a second chance
- Take advantage of an unexpected opportunity
- Make a deadline when you're running out of time
- Follow up in a thoughtful way after being offered an opportunity
- Make an impression as a finishing touch

ATTITUDE, STRATEGY, AND EXECUTION

Is the essence of getting scrappy found in one's attitude, a well-crafted strategy, or ultimately the execution of an effort? The answer is yes—all three!

I like to think I am scrappy. I feel like I have had a fairly consistent "attitude of scrappiness" for as long as I can remember. I have tried to embrace challenges, push myself to be creative, and forge ahead with optimism through the highs and lows of my career path. Maybe you feel this way too. Lots of people *feel* they are scrappy—and they're probably right. But that's just the beginning. It takes attitude, strategy, and execution to make things happen, and there are fundamental differences between all three:

Attitude: Having a scrappy *attitude* speaks to your mindset. It's the "fire in your belly" and a determined nature or spirit that can't really be quantified. Common denominators and distinct behavior patterns are clearly visible in the stories of scrappy people. Before taking action, their scrappy perspectives and mindset allowed them to view the obstacles in their path with curiosity and confidence rather than fear and defeat. A scrapper exhibits an active imagination, a penchant for risk taking, stubbornness, and a sense of appreciation, gratitude, and mindfulness.

Attitude is critical. Without the right attitude, it's virtually impossible to stay consistent in your effort or strategy. When you feel a little beaten up and tired, it's sheer will and a scrappy attitude that keep you committed to your vision. It often takes a bit of time to launch a scrappy effort, but getting into the right frame of mind is the first step.

Strategy: Coming up with a clever idea, a work-around, or a game-changing tactic is a key component of the scrappy philosophy. Sure, with the right attitude you can put in the effort, but it's the right *strategy* that can change the game to save you time, money, sanity, and more. A scrappy strategy encompasses all of your efforts—research, due diligence, and sweat equity. It's the product of all of the tactical planning necessary to achieve a specific goal. It's about rolling up your shirtsleeves, doing the day-to-day work, and committing your valuable time and energy to make something happen.

To craft a strategy, you will develop your approach to key decision makers, invest in the process, and cultivate your best ideas. One simple but critical component is simply showing up—being present and willing to get in the ring and do the work.

If your initial plan falls apart, your ability to morph your strategy along the way and stay the course is often what will pull you through. This is where your intuition, your ability to adapt, and your preparation help minimize losses and increase your wins.

Execution: Scrappy *execution* is about putting your plan of action into play. Upon execution, you will "put your tush on the line" and sometimes take real risks to reap significant rewards. If you want your circumstances to change, at some point you have to stop strategizing and launch.

The execution of a scrappy strategy transitions from planning into actual engagement, moving forward on a course of action you have developed (whether simple or elaborate). It's the "go" phase and typically happens when someone is motivated by a time-related circumstance, driving a person to engage his or her creativity in a groundbreaking or thought-provoking way. It can be an experiment or a mission of conviction.

You will find many examples of these elements of scrappiness throughout this book and see how the magic is in the mix—it's the combination of all three plus a dash of serendipity that makes it all work.

GETTING SCRAPPY HAS RANGE

The following three stories illustrate how getting scrappy can take many forms. They all feature scrappy people but are dramatically different in timing, pace, and personal investment. These stories show that scrappiness exists on a virtually endless spectrum of behaviors—from reserved and conservative to bold and brash and everything in between.

Consider the story of boutique owner Jennifer Matthey Riker, who experienced life-changing results after she decided to play big with her dating life. At the age of thirty-six, the self-described "serial entrepreneur" was single with no children but eager to get married and start a family. She was sensitive to the fact that her biological clock was ticking. As a marketing consultant with her own business, Jennifer had plenty of freedom and flexibility, but she wasn't meeting many eligible men. She worked from home and most of her clients were on the East Coast. She gave online dating a fair shake but found it too time consuming and not really suited to her personality. So she started brainstorming, trying to pinpoint the best places to go to meet the right kinds of guys. After all, Jennifer had a specific goal—to meet a man who wanted the same things she did. She eventually decided she needed to place herself in a setting where she could meet men naturally.

> *Although I didn't need the job, I took a sales position at Nordstrom, working two nights a week in the men's department. I figured it would be worth a try. The good news is after only two weeks, this gorgeous guy walked into the store. (He actually wasn't even there to shop but had walked through the building to get to a bookstore!) It was one of those moments where our eyes literally met across racks of clothes. He made up some excuse about needing a white shirt, and the rest is history.*

Today Jennifer and her husband are celebrating thirteen years of marriage and have two children. When she tells people how they met, the first response is laughter. The second is usually something like, "Wow, that was really smart of you!"

While Jennifer's illustration was a more personal reason to get scrappy, here's an example from a professional perspective. Donny Deutsch, chairman of Deutsch Inc., advertising agency, and host of the hit CNBC television show *The Big Idea with Donny Deutsch* has an incredible story of how early in his career, he convinced his father not to sell David Deutsch Associates but to instead give him an expanded role in the company and the chance to create his own brand with new accounts. To prove himself, he needed to show he could bring in significant clients and new business.

Donny set his sights on capturing the attention of the man in charge of awarding a huge advertising account for a regional car dealership, a story he describes in his book *Often Wrong, Never in Doubt*. He knew they would be competing with twenty other agencies for the account. He looked at the situation and asked himself, "How can we change the playing field and get the people on the buying side of the equation to say: 'I have to give these guys a chance.'" While sitting around brainstorming with his colleagues, Donny said, "Let's do something different. Outrageous. Out of the box. What can we send [the decision maker]?" He noted that, "fruit baskets and bottles of booze weren't going to cut it." Then one of his father's partners at the time came up with the idea of *used* car parts. Donny and the team got especially creative and became what I like to call "positive disrupters." They accomplished this by shipping a variety of individual car parts to the decision maker, each one accompanied by a different message. For instance, the headlight said, "We'll Give You Bright Ideas," while the fender promised, "We'll Protect Your Rear End," and the steering wheel pledged, "We'll Steer You in the Right Direction." They shipped one car part every half hour for a twelve-hour period to the man's home.

By the end of the day, Donny and his team had sent twenty-four car parts with twenty-four unique and memorable messages. Donny said, "It could have backfired. He could have been offended or felt intruded upon . . . but he thought the idea was so clever and so off the wall he said, 'I've got to go see these guys.'" The strategy was bold—and it worked. They made it into the finals and became one of the five agencies to pitch the business. Because of this scrappy effort, they became the favored underdog and ultimately got the deal.

The reason I love this illustration is because it shows how even a successful businessperson still had the need to get scrappy, meet a challenge, and make something happen when the pressure was on.

The final story is an example of getting scrappy over the long haul after numerous setbacks. You may not recognize the name Steven Schussler, CEO of Schussler Creative Inc., but you are probably familiar with his very popular theme restaurant Rainforest Café. Steve is one of the scrappiest people I know, with countless scrappy stories. He is open and honest about his wins and losses. This story about how he launched Rainforest Café is one of my favorites:

Steve first envisioned a tropical-themed family restaurant back in the 1980s, but unfortunately, he couldn't persuade anyone else to buy into the idea at the time. Not willing to give up easily, he decided to get scrappy and be "all in." To sell his vision, he transformed his own split-level suburban home into a living, mist-enshrouded rain forest to convince potential investors that the concept was viable. Yes, you read that correctly—he converted his own house into a jungle dwelling complete with rock outcroppings, waterfalls, rivers, and layers of fog and mist that rose from the ground. The jungle included a life-size replica of an elephant near the front door, forty tropical birds in cages, and a live baby baboon named Charlie. Steve shared the following details:

> Every room, every closet, every hallway of my house was set up
> as a three-dimensional vignette: an attempt to present my idea of
> what a rain forest restaurant would look like in actual opera-
> tion. . . . [I]t took me three years and almost $400,000 to get the

house developed to the point where I felt comfortable showing it to potential investors. . . . [S]everal of my neighbors weren't exactly thrilled to be living near a jungle habitat. . . .

On one occasion, Steve received a visit from the Drug Enforcement Administration. They wanted to search the premises for drugs, presuming he may have had an illegal drug lab in his home because of his huge residential electric bill. I imagine they were astonished when they discovered the tropical rain forest filled with jungle creatures.

Steve's plan was beautiful, creative, fun, and scrappy, but the results weren't coming as quickly as he would have liked. It took all of his resources, and he was running out of time and money to make something happen. (It's important to note that your scrappy efforts

An illustration of Steven Schussler's home Rainforest Café prototype

may not generate results immediately.) I asked Steve if he ever thought about quitting, how tight was the money really, and if there was a time factor, and he said, "Yes to all three! Of course I thought about quitting. I was running out of money and time."

Ultimately, Steve's plan succeeded. After many visits and more than two years later, gaming executive and venture capitalist Lyle Berman bought into the concept and raised the funds necessary to get the Rainforest Café up and running. The Rainforest Café chain became one of the most successful themed restaurants ever created, and continues that way under Landry's Restaurants and Tilman Fertitta's leadership. Today, Steve creates restaurant concepts in fantastic warehouses far from his residential neighborhood!

When you look at the stories of Jennifer, Donny, and Steve, you see three driven, imaginative people who chose to get scrappy to meet a major life goal. But their efforts were vastly different. Jennifer took an unorthodox approach to dating and initiated a bold yet classy plan to meet eligible men interested in marriage and family. Propelled by her scrappy attitude, she made a few simple changes and saw amazingly fast results that created a significant shift in her circumstances. With pressure mounting, Donny executed a wildly creative plan to demonstrate his ability to generate sales at his father's company and ultimately landed a big client. Steve's scrappy strategy was elaborate in scope, taking years to complete. His efforts to push through countless rejections worked beautifully *over time* and required patience, optimism, and attention to detail in a way that most people are not willing to commit.

So here's the next question: Is there a formula, or a proven set of steps, for building the perfect scrappy strategy? No, but there is a checklist that you will want to consider before you take action, which will be provided at the end of the book.

Sometimes you will have to wing it and get scrappy on the fly and in the moment. Other times you can sketch out a plan and your effort will follow a simple progression. There is no one specific formula. That's what keeps it interesting and creative.

As you will see in all of the examples in this book, getting scrappy is a bit of a wild ride, and each encounter unfolds in its own unique way. It's like surfing. You might learn the basic principles— how to paddle out, pull yourself up on the board, even stand up—but each wave is different. No two will ever be alike. Some are nice and long, and you can conquer them at a slow, rolling pace. Others are huge and fast and force you to drop in, use your best skills, and get out before you get killed. The more waves you take on, the better you get at maneuvering your way through the water.

In the book *The Hard Thing About Hard Things*, author Ben Horowitz points out that there is "no recipe for really complicated, dynamic situations. . . . That's the hard thing about hard things . . . there is no formula for dealing with them . . . but there are bits of advice and experience that can help with the hard things."

It's the same with getting scrappy. What makes this kind of effort stand out is the very fact that it can't be bottled and sold on a shelf. But we can learn from those who have gone before us and benefit from their experience.

Below you will find a quick road map of our journey. The content of this book will be divided into three sections exploring attitude, strategy, and execution. Here's how the chapters will unfold in the pages ahead:

Attitude

- Chapter 2: Mindset: Choose to Play Big
- Chapter 3: Deciding to Go Changes the Game

Strategy

- Chapter 4: Developing Your Scrappy Approach
- Chapter 5: Investing in the Process
- Chapter 6: Cultivating Scrappy Ideas

Execution

- Chapter 7: Risk, Mistakes, and Avoiding Failure
- Chapter 8: Scaling a Scrappy Culture and Strategy Within an Organization
- Chapter 9: Leaving Room for Serendipity
- Chapter 10: Executing Your Plan: Put Your Tush on the Line (Includes: Scrappy Strategy Action Checklist)

In each of these chapters we will explore ideas and strategies used successfully by others. The goal is not to copy these efforts, but rather to allow them to help trigger and stimulate your own ideas. At the end of each chapter you will be provided with an optional activity designed to help you better develop and implement your next scrappy effort.

At this point you may be wondering, "If I follow the counsel in this book and get scrappy in order to play big, will it work?" The answer to this question is: It really depends on you. Is your attitude scrappy? Do you have a strategy? When the time comes, will you move forward and execute?

Being scrappy is about making things happen, getting in the game and going for it. Let's play big! Use your imagination! What if your plan actually works? Imagine that.

REVIEW

- To be scrappy is to have the determination of a street fighter, to work smarter, to be willing to work harder when you need to, and to take risks and play big.
- Having a scrappy *attitude* speaks to your mindset. It's the "fire in your belly" and a determined nature or spirit that can't really be quantified.
- A scrappy *strategy* includes the effort and prep work required to put together an effective plan. It combines the due diligence, sweat equity, and tactical planning necessary to achieve a specific goal.
- Scrappy *execution* is about putting your plan of action into play. Upon execution, you will "put your tush on the line" and sometimes take real risks to reap significant rewards.
- Getting scrappy takes many forms, existing on a virtually endless spectrum of human behaviors.

What's Next: The first step in getting scrappy begins with having the right attitude. In the next section we will explore the significance of having the right mindset and why choosing to move forward is integral to the process.

Part 1
ATTITUDE

Having a scrappy attitude is characterized by your mindset and speaks to your fighting spirit. It's about the "fire in your belly" and a determined nature that can't really be quantified. This section is designed to help you adopt a scrappy attitude or enhance the one you already have. The next two chapters will examine attitude from two perspectives, showing you how to cultivate a scrappy mindset and explaining how simply "deciding to go" changes the game.

Chapter 2

MINDSET: CHOOSE TO PLAY BIG

ONE OF THREE THINGS COULD BE HAPPENING INSIDE YOUR mind right now. Option A: You're super fired up about being scrappy and are ready to get started! Option B: You're experiencing push-back, self-doubt, and maybe a bit of anxiety and fear at the prospect of taking action. Then, of course, there's Option C: a little bit of both.

This chapter will explore how a scrappy mindset requires you to address any limiting beliefs and common excuses that might be standing in your way and will teach you how to get comfortable with being uncomfortable. We will also look at a couple of examples of people whose scrappy attitudes led them to find unconventional solutions to deal with challenging situations.

Some of you might already have an active scrappy attitude, and this chapter can help you channel that energy and improve your overall execution. For others, such an attitude might be an entirely new mindset that will take time to develop.

At the end of this section on attitude, my hope is that you will come to understand the power you hold once you have the right mindset, make the choice to play bigger, and "decide to go."

> *If you want something badly enough you will find a way. If you don't, you will find an excuse.*
>
> **—Author unknown**

BREAKING DOWN COMMON EXCUSES

Part of developing a scrappy mindset is breaking through your own blocks and overcoming excuses. Let's say you want to get scrappy but you're on the fence. It's normal to think about all the ways it could go wrong, not work, or end up being a bad idea. Consider the story of David and Goliath. When David, who was by all accounts a scrawny shepherd boy, looked up at the giant Goliath, he might have thought to himself, "Hmmm, maybe this is not a good idea." Let's face it, his choice to forgo armor and the traditional weaponry could have easily ended up being a disaster. In addition, the people watching him probably thought to themselves, "I can't believe David is going in with nothing but a slingshot! I would never do that!" But David did. Relying on his strengths, he took a stand in the face of overwhelming odds, found a creative, yet clever solution, and won. That's the spirit of scrappy—moving forward in the face of adversity when most people would not.

In this life, excuses abound and most people will let you use them. In fact, there are many culturally acceptable excuses. To be fair, we all have our own blocks. Think about the scrappy individuals whose stories you have been reading. These people quelled the negative self-talk inside their heads. It wasn't easy, but they resisted the pull of excuses and ingrained patterns of behavior and embraced their creativity in new and sometimes frightening ways.

Expand your vision of what could really happen in your life and ask yourself a few "what if" questions before opting out. For example: If you could be, do, or have anything you wanted, what would you choose? Have you tried to get it? If so, what happened? If not, why not?

Could you try again? Will you try again? Sometimes we get in our own way.

Get Out of Your Own Way: You Can Dream Bigger, You're Not Too Young, Too Old, Too Inexperienced, Too Whatever

In conversations about getting scrappy in group settings, I have noticed that most people sincerely love to hear the stories about how their peers pushed through a barrier or landed a big client account—and they truly celebrate the wins! But when they get into a one-on-one conversation, they will quietly share their excuses—trying to explain why they're not doing what they really want to do or going after a big dream or goal. It's actually kind of normal. In fact, we all get good at what I call negative forecasting.

What is the number one excuse? It centers on the mysterious "they." The biggest, scariest threat always seems to be what "they" will think. (For example: They won't pick me. They already have a ton of great people on their team. They won't think I have enough experience, etc.) I'm not sure who "they" are, but this shadowy group certainly holds a lot of power over most of us. Too often, we start out already believing that whatever "they" might think, do, or say is true and justified, even before we really give ourselves a chance. And if "they" aren't the challenge—then we are, with our own limiting beliefs. These worries and suspicions come in myriad forms, but here are a few of the most common:

"I've tried once and failed, and it feels hopeless to try again."

"They already said no."

"I'm sure someone else has already done this."

"They are working with someone else, they aren't going to change."

"They will think I'm not good enough."

"They will see that I'm too old/young/inexperienced/ overqualified."

"I don't have a college degree, so I might as well not apply."

"I didn't go to the right schools."

"I'm already at the top of my game, so there's nowhere else for me to go."

"They will never give me a shot—they don't hire people with my (insert your limitation of choice)."

Are you worried that you don't have what it takes? In the book *Do Over*, Jon Acuff addresses this question poignantly with a very personal answer:

What if I don't have what it takes? The only thing more ex-hausting than chasing a dream is running away from one. I ran from the idea of writing for years and the question that haunted me most was, "What if I don't have what it takes?"

The tradeoff I was making when I allowed this question to win was: I would rather not try and not know I don't have what it takes—than try and know for certain. It's a career twist on the question, "Is it better to have loved and lost than to never have loved at all?" This is a fascinating fear because as many times as we encounter it, we never take the time to dissect it.

You're never going to know what may happen until you try. Giving in to excuses is what I call self-selecting out. It's when we are standing in a place where we could make something happen, but we take ourselves out of the equation. As my mentor Harvey Mackay says, "Don't say no for another person." That bit of advice changed my life, and I refer to it all the time. So step into yes.

Get Comfortable with Being Uncomfortable

You can fail at what you don't want, so you might as well take a chance on doing what you love!

—Jim Carrey

What are the motivations or challenges in your life leading you to want something different? I asked people I interviewed this simple question: "What pushed you to get scrappy?" The answer: They were typically feeling some kind of discomfort. Maybe they were bored, frustrated, angry, or just wanting a big change and they were irritated enough to push past all of the excuses. You can learn to welcome discomfort and even use it as a tool to make something new and different happen when you have an inspired intention.

It's the old adage about the oyster: "The oyster without an irritation creates no pearl."

Think of it this way: An oyster experiencing irritation inside its shell or an attack from the outside creates a pearl sac to seal off the irritant. The end result—a beautiful pearl—is the by-product of an adaptive immune system–like function. Similarly, I say that getting scrappy is the by-product of our efforts to combat an irritation or solve a problem.

It may be easier to get your head around the idea of managing your fears than to overcome them, and that's fine. Overcoming your fears may take a while. Initially, you may just have to get comfortable with being uncomfortable and learn to manage them better. These feelings will come up each and every time you take on a bigger task or challenge through various stages of life. For example, even though I have been in the speaking industry for over twenty years, my heart starts racing the moment I walk out onstage for a big speaking engagement. I have to say a little prayer, remind myself to breathe, remember that I'm prepared for the moment, and then I go. I can't say that I have overcome the anxiety and pressure I feel in those moments, but I have made every effort to manage them and coexist with these feelings and "bring my A game."

I agree with the wisdom of Elizabeth Gilbert, who said in her work *Big Magic*, "Creativity can only coexist alongside Fear . . . and you must learn to accept them both, if you want to invent things."

She suggests that we move forward, "walking right beside Creativity and Fear, who are enmeshed forever, limping along, definitely a little weird-looking, but forever advancing despite each other."

Beautifully said. Let's embrace the discomfort and accept that it can be a catalyst to move us forward.

Intentionally Seeking Out Challenges

A scrappy attitude takes awareness to sustain and has the potential to affect virtually every corner of your life, from personal to professional and everything in between. It's important to note that being scrappy is not limited to career milestones such as landing a game-changing account, a major promotion, or a better job. In fact, your decision to get scrappy might have nothing to do with improving your financial circumstances. It could grow out of your desire to live your life in a specific way—more spontaneously, more on the edge—or to intentionally seek out challenges.

A beautiful example of this is Beck Bamberger, CEO of BAM Communications. This journalist and PR wizard is "obsessed with experience."

> *It's the only thing we leave the planet with, and our collection of experiences shapes our entire lives. You can buy stuff, you can collect things, but what tells your story and fills your life is a collective of experiences. Time is the ultimate luxury. Experience is the best currency we've got.*

To that end, Beck committed to personally engage in an entire year of uncomfortable experiences. The goal was to push herself beyond her own physical and mental limits, breaking through internal barriers and accelerating personal growth.

Being uncomfortable is a function of fear multiplied by novelty. If you want to get better at being uncomfortable with a particular situation, then you need to diminish your fear around it or lower the novelty of the experience. You have to change your mind—rewire all of those subjective thoughts or opinions formed during your upbringing—and intentionally place yourself in the situation repeatedly to weaken its power. That's how you feel less uncomfortable with anything.

Uncomfortable is very personal. What is uncomfortable for me might be easy and natural for someone else. It depends on the person. Collecting these experiences isn't a competition against others. For me, it's more about a commitment to self-expansion.

Beck has amassed quite a list. We're talking stuff that most people would never consider. In October 2015, she completed a weekend survival course that had her living in the woods with only a sleeping bag, knife, and water bottle. Beck learned to make fire with nothing but sticks, to boil water with just a rock and a Ziploc bag, construct a shelter she slept in for the whole night, and build a trap for small game. "All in all, despite my prolonged dislike of camping or [as it were] 'surviving,' I'm glad I did it, and I might consider some more advanced courses."

Other uncomfortable experiences on her growing list include working with the dead, particularly in the area of cremation and embalming.

A few months before her survival adventure, Beck tackled a poetry slam. She wrote and performed a poem in front of three hundred people onstage—snapping and all. (Snapping is used instead of clapping at poetry venues. It started during the 1950s in Greenwich Village when beatniks gathered in dingy basement apartments to read their poetry. They snapped their fingers to show appreciation on a quieter scale so as not to disturb the residents living upstairs.)

> First, I am not an artsy-fartsy, let-me-read-my-journal theatrical type, so this wasn't my usual jam. I had serious help from my pal Adam In-q. As many of you know, Adam is a savant of poetry who gets hired by the likes of Nike and Disney to recite his stuff. In short, I worked with the best in the business.
>
> So every Tuesday night, about 300 people gather to hear open mic poems at this little theater in West Hollywood. I would say the average age is twenty. Let's just say I missed the memo on wearing my high tops and black hoodie with bedazzled phrases, but it was cool. Part of being in these uncomfortable experiences is knowing fully that you completely and patently stick out. Also, as soon as I saw about 200 people waiting in line to get in, I knew I couldn't back out. (You know you're in an uncomfortable experience when you have that glaring moment that rings out something in your head like, "Nah. Don't really want to do this. Nope.")

What went down inside that theater certainly wasn't amateur hour. Many of the kids who performed shared outstanding prose about intense topics ranging from rape to suicide. Beck's poem was about talking to people on a bus—so, a bit of a different flare. She covered rehab, single motherhood, salaries, and the like based on her conversations with the people she had met.

Overall, mega thumbs up on this experience. I wanted to be completely, utterly out of my element and exposed in front of an unfamiliar audience. Even better, it was an audience of people I often perceived as judgy and fickle with acceptance. Going in, I was asking myself, "Will I find this crowd accepting? If I bomb, will I even care?" The lesson I got was that you have to own what you're presenting. I'm certainly not a spoken word artist like the people I watched, but I can always do my best. So I did. I think the audience knew that too and politely accepted what I offered.

Ultimately, Beck discovered that it's possible to actually *practice being comfortable with being uncomfortable* in the same way one might practice for a marathon by running miles at a time.

It's a mental muscle you have to flex over and over again in order to master your discomfort with a particular situation or experience. Now that I've had several of these experiences, I've found the challenge of growing a business with dozens of clients and employees to be, quite frankly, less daunting.

WHAT PUSHING PAST EXCUSES LOOKS LIKE

Getting scrappy doesn't guarantee you a win, but if you plan well it can give you another opportunity or significantly improve your chances for success. If your plan didn't work the first time, change the plan, not the goal. If you want to work in the music industry, but you just don't have the pipes to be a vocalist, perhaps you could get really good at managing singers and musicians. Maybe you're a baseball enthusiast but not major league player material. Why not try announcing for a team? What if you want to be a pilot but have claustrophobia? Maybe you design flight simulators, a choice that keeps you working in the field you love but uses your talents in a different way.

Consider the story of Ross Bernstein, now a best-selling sports author, who took his dream of being a college hockey player for the University of Minnesota Golden Gophers and morphed it into what ultimately became his dream job and true calling.

Ross grew up in Minnesota imagining how amazing it would be to play hockey for the Golden Gophers. He wasn't recruited out of high school, but when he finally became a student at the university he made friends with some of the hockey players who helped him "walk on" to try out for the team. For Ross, this was a dream come true. One day during tryouts he decided he would attempt to make an impression on the coaches.

The star player and team captain, a guy named Todd Richards, was skating down the ice, and he was wearing this really weird jersey. It was all white, with this big red cross (like a target). And I thought, "You know what? I'm gonna take out the star player." I equated it to the first day of prison, where you've got to shank the biggest dude in the yard the first day, or really bad things are going to happen to you. So, I took him out and flattened him. I don't remember a lot from there because one of the

*assistant coaches, a former goon in the NHL, flattened me. When
I literally came to, he had his hand around my neck and the other
hand in a fist and he was screaming at me, "You idiot! Our star
player's wearing a red cross jersey. That means he's injured!"*

As a result, Ross was cut during tryouts in preseason. In that one moment, his dream was dead. He was devastated.

Was there any way to recover from this? He could have argued that he tried and failed. He could have given up on pursuing his dream. But no . . .

In a bizarre sequence of events, he heard about a new slot opening up for the team mascot, Goldie the Gopher. Initially the idea seemed crazy. But in order to stay close to the team, Ross decided to morph his plan. Being the mascot might not have been his original goal, but he went for it.

*I made lemonade out of lemons by changing the plan a bit. (I
got to be with the cheerleaders, which was awesome.) I still got to
practice with the team, which was huge. I still got to be a part of
it all, and I got to entertain ten thousand uber-enthusiastic and
crazy fun fans every weekend.*

Ross took on his new role with humor and a little edge, often creating mischief—like the time he threw Kraft cheese singles at the Wisconsin band—and pushing the boundaries of a mascot, which always seemed to amuse his audience. During his senior year, he was even approached by a publisher who wanted him to write a book about all of his antics.

Ultimately, Ross morphed his plan but kept his eyes on his overall goal of staying connected to his beloved Golden Gophers. He capitalized on his experience by writing a book about the sport, his mascot adventures, the team, and more, which led to a celebrated career as a published author and business speaker.

Another good example of stepping into "yes" and not self-selecting out, even though the odds were against him, is the story of my friend Greg Hague. Greg is living proof that you're never too old to reach for your dream.

For as long as Greg could remember, he had dreamed of being a courtroom attorney. After he graduated from law school, however, his father, who suffered from emphysema, asked him to help out in his Cincinnati real estate business, which took him off plan.

Forty years later, Greg was in real estate, but practicing law was still "the dream." He finally decided to do something about it and sit for the bar. "If not then, when? I wasn't going to get any younger. It was 2009, the real estate market was in turmoil; what could be a better time to go for it?" Greg was sixty years old and knew most people thought he was too old. They thought he was crazy and it would be nearly impossible for him to pass the bar when he had graduated from law school so many years ago. (There "they" are again!)

I faced dark days of doubt. Even my youngest son said at Christmas in 2009, "Dad, you'd be a god if you passed the bar exam. It's okay if you want to give up, I will still love you." When he said that I knew I had to get it done. The thing is I had no idea of the magnitude of the undertaking, and the odds against me even passing.

I was scheduled to take the ridiculously difficult (failure rate of 30–40 percent) two-day Arizona bar exam in 4½ months. And, I hadn't looked at a law book in over 35 years (since I graduated from law school). Most every other applicant had just finished three years of intense law school study.

He began looking at all the traditional study methods—groups, outlines, notes, laborious reading—and immediately realized they weren't going to work. He had to get creative with his study skills if he was going to pass the exam. Greg vowed to succeed—even if it meant pulling all-nighters. "I flat out made up my mind I was going to pass."

He took one week to experiment with different methods of absorbing and recalling material and eventually devised a learning system he calls L4X. He applied it diligently over the next four and a half months, using it to learn twice the information in half the time.

Greg sat for the bar and then motorcycled through Africa to regain his sanity while awaiting the results. When he returned home, he learned that he not only passed the exam but received the number one score in the state!

Many have since said I was the oldest person in the nation to ever score number one on a state bar exam. After the results were published, my story was featured in the newspaper, on radio and television news. It was newsworthy because no one had ever done what I did. No one at my age with so little time to study had ever scored number one on a bar exam.

Both Ross Bernstein and attorney Greg Hague are real-life examples of people who got scrappy to work through "culturally acceptable excuses" or roadblocks for quitting. Most people would have given up entirely in Ross's situation, but he turned everything around by morphing his plan and now he is so grateful that things worked out the way they did. Most people would have given up the dream of passing the bar at Greg's age and said, "Ah, I am too old. That ship has sailed." But the person who has a scrappy mindset finds a work-around and makes something happen to change their circumstances.

So what if you try and fail—the first time? At the end of the day, life happens, and sometimes even when you go for a dream you come up short. Failure is a part of life, but it doesn't have to obliterate your dreams.

Whatever the block, you can be sure that the scrappy individuals in this book experienced many of the same frustrations along their journeys that you might be facing. They just found another way, another path, and designed a new plan.

Give Yourself Permission to Go

You can do this! Give yourself permission to rise above what my good friend entrepreneur Brad McMillen calls "a sea of sameness"—that overwhelming tide of uniform gestures and behaviors:

> *People are bored with the same song and dance. People want to be wooed. They want to see some scrappy behavior. They appreciate it. They celebrate it. Whether or not they choose you, they remember you. In the end, you have nothing to lose. If you think*

you will look like a fool, who cares? The big fish thinks you're a weirdo because you sent a basket of fruit? Your life will still be the same by doing nothing. If, however, you choose to stand out, to make a difference, you might actually get what you're after.

It's okay to buck the norm. Sure, typical educational and professional settings have not encouraged us to be scrappers. Their job is to teach us to work within the standard protocol and rules. And that's okay . . . but it's boring! Intuitively you know this. Yes, getting scrappy might feel a bit awkward in the beginning, but when you give yourself permission to go and to play bigger, it can work—and whether it works or not, it's more fun.

A SHOUT-OUT TO THE CATERPILLAR

We delight in the beauty of the butterfly, but rarely admit the changes it has gone through to achieve that beauty.

—Maya Angelou

Part of my work as a speaker and trainer is to deliver small group workshops on how to give more effective presentations. People are not always excited to take this class, and I get it. They are pleased with the end result, but getting there requires working through varying degrees of reluctance and resistance.

When an instructor is coaching adults and asks them to participate in a transformative drill that will teach them how to build and deliver more polished presentations, that instructor will receive a certain amount of push-back. Sure, ideologically we all know that training, practicing, and developing our skills helps to make us better professionals. However, when we actually have to engage in the training activities, most of us wouldn't call it fun. So when I start to hear the grumble just before we execute a drill, I share an analogy about the plight of the caterpillar.

Imagine for a moment that you're a caterpillar. Everybody is encouraging you to be a butterfly, but maybe you're comfortable, content, and not feeling the need to do anything different. You're happy being a caterpillar.

Why take the risk of throwing yourself off a branch, to hang by a string upside down for three to four weeks? Then go through some kind of unknown and probably painful metamorphosis—for what? To potentially emerge as a butterfly? What if you aren't sure you want to be a butterfly?

Maybe others have even praised you for being the best caterpillar ever.

I imagine that at some point, the caterpillar had to seriously think about this. Maybe he even thought, "Nope, I'm not doing it! Butterflies aren't that cool anyway. Caterpillars should all be happy as they are." Maybe some of his caterpillar friends agreed. (Not to mention that he could be risking death. I mean, how many caterpillars even make it through the journey?)

On the other hand, maybe he had friends who said, "Come on, let's just do it. It will be an adventure."

Somewhere, in all of the doubt and anxiety, the caterpillar realizes he *does* want to be a butterfly; he was just scared and felt a bit intimidated. In that moment, he takes the leap to "make things happen" and goes for it.

The caterpillar puts everything on the line! He doesn't listen to excuses. He just does what's next to become a butterfly. The commitment to complete the journey and come out the other side is the part of this story that should be praised and celebrated. But it's not. All you ever really hear about is how beautiful the butterfly is, but if the caterpillar hadn't been willing to make that chrysalis, the butterfly would never have come to be. As George Carlin said, "The caterpillar does all of the work, but the butterfly gets all the publicity."

Every caterpillar has the potential to be a butterfly if it chooses. Each of us has the potential to be, do, or have whatever we desire. That said, just like the caterpillar, we eventually must decide what we really want, manage our own fears, and choose to accept the risk, endure the pain, and take action.

Let's agree, for the remainder of this book, that you will put your excuses aside and get comfortable with being uncomfortable. You're going to cultivate your scrappy mindset, move forward in the face of adversity, and push your creativity to new levels. Don't worry if you don't have all the answers. Once you choose to play big, the answers will come.

REVIEW

- Part of developing a scrappy mindset is breaking through your own blocks and overcoming excuses. Sometimes you have to get out of your own way.
- You can learn to welcome discomfort and even use it as a tool to make something new and different happen when you have an inspired intention.

- A scrappy attitude takes awareness to sustain, and it has the potential to affect virtually every corner of your life, from personal to professional and everything in between. It could grow out of your desire to live your life in a specific way—more spontaneously, more on the edge—or to intentionally seek out challenges.

- Getting scrappy doesn't guarantee you a win, but if you plan well it can give you another opportunity or significantly improve your chances of success. If your plan didn't work the first time, morph the plan, not the goal. Failure is part of life, but it doesn't have to obliterate your dreams.

Chapter Activity: Take some time to expand your vision of what could really happen in your life and ask yourself a few "what if" questions. For example: If you could be, do, or have anything you wanted, what would you choose? Have you tried to get it? If so, what happened? If not, why not?

How can you shift your mindset, tap into your fighting spirit and scrappy attitude, and try again? It may be uncomfortable at first to play bigger.

Choose one activity that makes you feel uncomfortable. Do it and explore the idea of getting comfortable with being uncomfortable.

What's Next: In the next chapter we will explain why it's essential for you to choose to be "all in" and decide to go.

Bonus Scrappy
Success Story #1

GETTING SCRAPPY TO
TURN THINGS AROUND

FOR SOME PEOPLE, GETTING SCRAPPY ISN'T OPTIONAL—IT'S their only play. For one reason or another, getting scrappy is the only thing standing between them and absolute disaster. Susan Sly, a successful entrepreneur and passionate philanthropist, knows a thing or two about finding yourself in this position.

Susan met her greatest challenge on January 13, 2000, when she was diagnosed with multiple sclerosis. At only twenty-seven years old—with a husband, a young daughter, and a demanding business—it was a devastating blow. Three days later her marriage fell apart. She was heartbroken. Four months after that, Susan arrived at the health club she owned with her husband to teach a spinning class and, surrounded by her students, found a padlock on the door. The club had been shut down because of unpaid taxes. "This was the lowest point in my life. I had lost everything."

In that moment, Susan knew it was up to her to change her

circumstances. Quitting was never really acceptable because of her daughter, so she chose not only to survive but to excel.

That day I was locked out of the club, I didn't know how, but I knew I was going to find a way to turn this whole situation around. I knew it was my responsibility, even in the face of illness, to get up every day and put one foot in front of the other and make it happen.

She moved in with her brother-in-law, intent on rebuilding her life from scratch. It was a hard road. Her MS had her slurring her words, dropping things, and battling a persistent brain fog. But she was all in and focused, with very little indecision. After all, when you're living on someone's couch, you're pretty much out of time. She didn't do anything fancy, just good old-fashioned scrappy effort.

I called every celebrity I had ever trained when I had been a personal trainer. I got letters of recommendation and went in for a job interview at Bally Total Fitness. I did not tell them I was sick, and I said, "No matter what happens I will become the number one sales producer in this company." I got the job, and I ended up becoming the top sales manager out of 444 clubs!

An inspiring story, to be sure, but how did Susan actually *turn things around?* Was it just a tenacious positive attitude? Was it simple determination? Or was it that delicate yet powerful combination of scrappy attitude, effort, and strategy aimed at changing the game and playing big? What is clear is that Susan walked toward the obstacle in her path—not away from it. She had to meet the challenge because all other doors were closed to her. In fact, she had closed them herself.

What I have learned from all I have been through is that no matter your goal, you have to make the commitment to being all in. Once I walk through a door, all other doors close and there are locks on those doors. Padlocks. Because I'm not going backward. It's like losing weight. When it comes to losing weight, you know you're all in when you get rid of your fat clothes. Keeping the fat clothes is keeping the safe door open.

Susan strongly dislikes and distrusts the safe door.

When you're sad or hurt, your first instinct is to choose the safe door, but the safe door is the most unsafe door. I think playing small is the most unsafe thing we can do. People who play small are so in their head. They think they're keeping themselves safe, but it's not safe to be in a space where day in and day out you're beating yourself up thinking about what could have been or what you should be doing as opposed to just going forward and doing it. To me, there's nothing safe about that.

Bottom line, Susan's focus on her one clear option—to regain her life—simply pushed aside her fear of failure. She tapped into her fighting spirit, took some risks, got scrappy, and changed the game.

Now when I set a huge goal for myself and truly go for it—no matter what it is—I feel it's always a win. I feel I can't really fail because no matter where I end up, I've evolved and that new place gives me a new vantage point, and that's better than the old view. So it's always a win.

Chapter 3

DECIDING TO GO CHANGES THE GAME

NOW THAT WE'VE GOT YOUR EXCUSES OUT OF THE WAY, THE goal of this chapter is to explain *why* it will be necessary for you to commit to being "all in." Deciding to go is a choice. This is a key component of engaging your scrappy attitude. I don't know how long it will take—days, months, or years—for you to reach your goal, but nothing will ever happen if you don't step into the challenge.

There is more going on than you might think behind the clever stories you have been reading in this book. There's an explanation for why and how some of these people came up with their inventive ideas, and it's not just luck. A real, measurable, and repeatable shift happens when you go "all in" on a specific challenge. It can be duplicated and everyone has the ability to get creative and innovative, and tap into some new ideas. And when you do, you get results.

In this chapter we will discuss how *deciding* to get scrappy disrupts your brain's normal thinking pattern, activating a shift in your mind that helps stimulate creativity. Then we will explore three elements necessary to produce breakthroughs. We will also examine the key conditions that, when combined, create an atmosphere in which scrappy people and scrappy attitudes excel.

How does deciding to go change the game? It works in the same way as a railroad switch.

At various points along a train track, rails have switches to divert a train from one track to another. The act of "deciding to go" and taking on a specific challenge works like a railroad switch. Somehow it activates a trigger in your brain, diverting it to a new route and pushing past old pathways. I don't know how this works. It just does.

COMMIT AND THE IDEAS WILL COME

The fascinating part about *choosing* to get scrappy is that the chances of coming up with a cool idea before you make that decision are slim. It's only after you have committed to meeting the challenge and said, "Hey, I'm all in!" that you open yourself up to creative, inspired thought. When I asked successful scrappy individuals how they came up with their ideas, here's what they said:

> "I was feeling the pressure. I knew I had to do something so I started playing with options in my mind. I just thought, 'What am I going to do?' And then, when I was driving and I saw an advertisement on the back of a truck, it triggered a random idea. Somehow it just came to me."

> "It just popped into my head after a bunch of other weird thoughts while I was running."

"I woke up in the middle of the night and wrote it down."

"I thought of it in the shower."

"I was at the gym in my Zumba class."

"When I finally took a break from thinking about it and I was working on my son's homework, something clicked—I put two and two together."

"After watching a movie, I had an epiphany."

"In a brainstorming session with my team, we were all exhausted and it started as a joke. Then we played around with it and the rest is history."

Have you ever experienced a similar awakening?

Scrappy people step into challenges and their brains join them, providing answers they couldn't begin to foresee but hoped would come. The ideas don't come first, the commitment does—and it doesn't usually happen right away. There's no specific time line for how long it will take for your brain to come up with a solution. It will happen when it happens.

DECIDING TO PLAY BIG STIMULATES IDEAS

Research suggests you are actually capable of thinking differently and more resourcefully because of the need to get scrappy—whether it's because of outside pressures or your own choice. The operative word here is "need." When your brain needs a solution, it will seek one out and find it.

Consider something we touched on in the introduction to this book. Some of the most interesting parts of scrappy stories occur during the journey, not just at the end. These individuals unknowingly stimulated their creativity to navigate the challenges in their path. It's the choices they made at the various turning points that changed the game. Something happened the moment they decided to do something big (or at least big for them) that created a mental shift. So how does it work?

To answer this question, I spoke with my brilliant friend Stephen Shapiro. He spent the first fifteen years of his career at the consulting firm Accenture, the last years leading a twenty-thousand-person innovation practice. Since 2001, the year he left consulting, he's been speaking about innovation around the world. Stephen explained:

> *The brain is wired to minimize loss . . . [and] to keep you alive. [It] makes the assumption that because you were alive yesterday, what you did previously is safe. Therefore, repeating the past is good for survival. As a result, doing things differently, even if it seems like an improvement, is risky. Perpetuating past behaviors, from the brain's reptilian perspective, is the safest way. This is why innovation is difficult for most individuals and organizations.*

Put another way, the brain wants its problems and predicaments solved first because it can't deal with anything new or different until they are addressed. The brain has no incentive to come up with new ideas if it doesn't have to. As long as your brain knows you have another out, it will always be content with keeping you alive by coming up with the same ideas that it used before.

This suggests that when you decide to get scrappy, a shift occurs and seems to unlock a door. Once that new door opens, you are more capable than ever of getting innovative because your brain has been activated to manage discomfort or challenges first. You're able to work on a new, perhaps more advanced, level with heightened energy and focus. It's that initial commitment, that literal act of saying, "I'm going for it!" that stimulates your mind in new and clever ways and ultimately leads to the generation of fresh ideas.

Let's go back to the Greg Hague story.

1. He had a huge goal, which was to pass the Arizona state bar exam.
2. There was a limited time frame as he had only four and a half months to study.
3. He was all in: "I flat out made up my mind I was going to pass." He decided to go despite the odds.
4. He had to figure out a way to learn a ton of information in a short period of time. His brain adapted, shifted, and developed an entirely new learning system in order to absorb more material, which helped him to pass the Arizona bar and get the top score in the state.

It's weird, right? But it happened.

Maybe you have a chance at a big opportunity and you want to *win*. Maybe a competitor is about to steal your best client and you have one shot to save the deal. Whatever your circumstances are, once you accept the challenge before you, your brain—somehow, someway—gets on board and has your back. As you boldly step onto the path of a challenge instead of retreating, your brain will change course to adapt.

The solution your brain comes up with may be a super quick and easy fix. For example, a simple act of kindness could be all that was needed to bridge a gap and keep things moving forward with a decision maker. Other scenarios require greater exploration, homework, and planning.

What happens if the stakes are high and you don't have a lot of time? Ultimately you have to do the best you can with what you have got.

Apollo 13

Let's revisit a moment in American history in which actual survival was at stake. Whether or not you're familiar with the amazing story of the *Apollo 13* mission to the moon, I trust you will be able to appreciate the following example.

In 1970, a team of NASA scientists and engineers was faced with the nearly impossible task of getting the damaged *Apollo 13* spacecraft patched up and the astronauts aboard it safely back home. The clock was ticking and dozens of brilliant scientists were scrambling to find a scrappy solution in a true life-or-death situation.

At fifty-five hours and forty-six minutes in, the ship's mission had been going well. The astronauts had adjusted to weightlessness and had even broadcast a forty-nine-minute TV special showing the people back on Earth what their life was like in space. At the end, Commander Jim Lovell spoke: "This is the crew of *Apollo 13* wishing everybody there a nice evening, and we're just about ready to close out our inspection of *Aquarius* and get back for a pleasant evening in *Odyssey*. Good night."

Nine minutes later, one of the spaceship's oxygen tanks exploded. Shortly afterward, the other oxygen tank failed. Electricity went out, leaving the astronauts without access to light and water, 200,000 miles from Earth, with no shuttle or rescue ship capable of being sent up with additional parts or to take them back home.

With the ship's oxygen rapidly disappearing, NASA and the three stranded astronauts—Commander Jim Lovell, command module pilot Jack Swigert, and lunar module pilot Fred Haise—had to power down the command module and move into the attached lunar module to survive. While they conserved water—each man drinking only six ounces daily—and turned off all noncritical systems, Mission Control managed to figure out how to charge the command module's batteries with power from the lunar module.

The next concern was the removal of carbon dioxide from the lunar module. According to NASA's Web site: "There were enough lithium hydroxide canisters, which remove carbon dioxide from the spacecraft, but the square canisters from the command module were not compatible with the round openings in the lunar module environmental system." After a day and a half of the astronauts' sharing the lunar module, the carbon dioxide had built up to a dangerous level.

On the ground in Houston, NASA scientists gathered the same parts available to the astronauts on board and began to brainstorm. They had to use what the astronauts had at their disposal—the pieces and parts on the ship. They collaborated. They argued. They pushed their intellects beyond any point they'd ever imagined. In the end, with raw talent and ingenuity, they devised a way to attach the command module canisters to the lunar module system by simply using plastic bags, cardboard, and tape. Those fixes ultimately gave the crew the time it needed to solve the larger problem of navigating safely back to Earth. Their work was a success, and the *Apollo 13* crew "splashed down gently in the Pacific Ocean near Samoa" on April 17, 1970.

Under normal circumstances, it's highly unlikely that any of those scientists would have invented a fix using plastic bags or

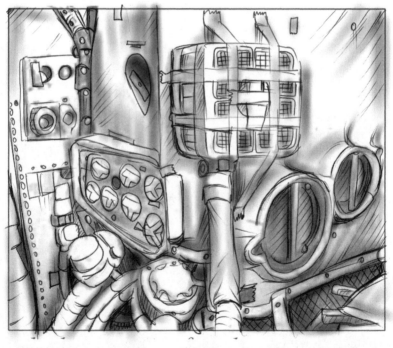

An illustration of the Apollo 13 fix (complete with duct tape) of making a square canister fit into a round hole

cardboard. It's unlikely they would have been able to come up with a plan so quickly had lives not been on the line. But they knew they had no choice but to come up with a solution. They decided to go, and then the answers came.

To be sure, most of us are not going to have to bring a stranded spacecraft safely back home. It's an amazing story that perfectly illustrates how even the brightest minds sometimes have to get out of their normal thinking patterns, step away from their brains' traditional pathways, and go back to the most rudimentary, yet dynamic solutions. That's scrappy.

AN ATMOSPHERE OF INNOVATION

All of this might be a lot to absorb, and you may be a little skeptical. The idea that a reaction in your brain takes place when you commit to getting scrappy could even seem mysterious and difficult to believe. But it's real, and its effectiveness has been proven and replicated by the Pentagon's Defense Advanced Research Projects Agency, or DARPA.

If you aren't familiar with DARPA, I encourage you to watch a popular TED talk available online for free at TED.com called "From Mach-20 Glider to Hummingbird Drone," delivered by an impressive woman named Regina Dugan, former director of DARPA.

Since its creation in 1958—in response to the Soviet Union's launch of *Sputnik*—DARPA's teams have had an unprecedented number of breakthroughs. The agency's innovations have included the Internet, stealth technology, global positioning satellites, and unmanned aerial vehicles. It's not the largest or most well-funded federal agency, but it might be the most focused. DARPA's accomplishments are all the more impressive given that its programs last an average of three to five years, employ fewer than three hundred people, and operate on an annual budget of about $3 billion. Writing about DARPA for the *Harvard Business Review*, Dugan and former deputy director Kaigham J. Gabriel described the agency this way: "With its unconventional approach, speed, and effectiveness, DARPA has created a 'special forces' model of innovation."

What makes DARPA tick is its commitment to creating an atmosphere specifically suited to produce breakthroughs where leading minds are encouraged to embrace a model of learning balanced on three crucial elements:

> *Ambitious goals: . . . The presence of an urgent need for an application creates focus and inspires greater genius. . . .*
>
> *Temporary project teams: [finite time frames] . . . These projects are not open-ended research programs. Their intensity, sharp focus, and finite time frame make them attractive to the highest-caliber talent, and the nature of the challenge inspires unusual levels of collaboration.*
>
> *Independence: . . . By charter, DARPA has autonomy in selecting and running projects. Such independence allows the organization to move fast and take bold risks and helps it persuade the best and brightest to join.*

DARPA establishes an urgent need, employs advanced thinkers for a short duration, and provides them with the autonomy to take bold risks. The result? Amazing scientific and technological advances.

Apply the DARPA Model to Your Own Scrappy Efforts

There are many similarities that parallel the conditions for getting scrappy with the elements of the DARPA model. What could happen if you knew how to tap into this creative surge by design like a DARPA team?

If you look carefully at the scrappy stories we've discussed so far, you will see that many of them include the three primary elements of the model. Those same conditions unfold organically in each situation. Not just in the Greg Hague story or the *Apollo 13* example, but even going back to the Girl Scout story in chapter 1. When these conditions combine, they create an atmosphere in which scrappy people with scrappy attitudes thrive.

Imagine that it is possible to apply the DARPA model on a smaller scale to a situation you are facing to *intentionally* stimulate your brain to get scrappy. You can set an ambitious goal, give yourself a limited amount of time in which to act, and resolve to go all in to succeed.

What might this look like for you?

Ambitious Goal: You might not be trying to create a new kind of stealth technology, but your goal could certainly be ambitious for you or where you are right now in your life. Danielle Lei set a big goal for herself—to sell a lot of Girl Scout cookies. What is your reason for getting scrappy? What is your goal? With total clarity of your mission comes a freedom to get as creative as possible and do everything you can to succeed—within professional and ethical boundaries of course.

Temporary Project Teams/Finite Time Frame: You might not have a large team of people to work with, but neither did Danielle. She and her mom turned out to be a great team of two and came up with a pretty scrappy idea that worked well for their goal. They had to work within the short time period of the cookie selling cycle against a great deal of competition.

Independence: Ultimately, it's up to you. You have the freedom to creatively build a strategic plan and execute it. Danielle had the freedom to execute in her own unique way, by setting up a Girl Scout cookie stand in a favorable environment in order to reach her goal.

Whatever your goal is, you're not crazy to try, but you would be crazy to try without putting some thought into it. Let's put it all together. Below is one more story that illustrates how the DARPA model organically parallels the actions of a scrappy individual who made things happen despite the odds.

BOB COSTAS AND A CASE OF BRATS AND SAUCE

Best-selling author and speaker Joe Sweeney is a firm believer that scrappiness often trumps persistence. About twenty years ago, he was the president of the Wisconsin Sports Authority, an agency that spurred economic development through the promotion of sports. One of the agency's board members wanted well-known NBC reporter Bob Costas to emcee its upcoming Wisconsin Sports Hall of Fame dinner, which would be attended by about three thousand people. Sweeney began by doing some research, networking with colleagues, and then contacting Costas directly to make his request, but Costas said he was simply too busy. Sweeney could have stopped there. He had a culturally acceptable excuse—Costas gave him a firm no. But Sweeney wasn't ready to back down. On the contrary, he decided to go all in and get a little scrappy.

Not one to give up easily, a few days later, Sweeney heard Costas announcing a baseball game in Milwaukee and made a point to really listen to the details of the conversations throughout the game. He heard Costas raving about the Milwaukee bratwurst and also the special stadium sauce that goes along with it. That triggered Sweeney's imagination and he got an idea to try again, this time sending a case of brats along with a second request to be the emcee. He had nothing to lose except for the expense of the brats and the postage.

Unfortunately, nothing happened. Silence. Crickets. No response. So Sweeney decided to make a third attempt and sent his request to Costas along with a case of the special sauce. Still nothing. Time was running out and the pressure was on. Sweeney still really wanted to make it happen, but his kind gestures and gifts were not making any impact or changing Costas's response. Now what? During a meeting Sweeney had with Governor Tommy Thompson, Thompson asked him if there was anything he could do to help. Sweeney asked the governor if he would be willing to write a letter to Costas as well, repeating the request for him to emcee the event.

Fortunately, this cumulative effort softened Costas on his decision and he changed his mind. Ultimately, he even complimented Joe Sweeney on his classy and creative efforts.

Final result: Costas served as the master of ceremonies at the Wisconsin Sports Hall of Fame dinner, where he actually recounted this entire sequence of events in his opening speech.

When faced with his ambitious goal—persuading Bob Costas to be an emcee—Sweeney was all in and decided to go. With only a short amount of time at his disposal, he brainstormed and researched with a higher level of focus than usual. Finally, as president of the Wisconsin Sports Authority, he had the freedom to be bold and take a few risks. As a result, Sweeney got his breakthrough and achieved his goal.

If you would like to see the Bob Costas presentation about Joe Sweeney's efforts, you can find the video "Joe Sweeney Testimonial/ American Sportscaster Bob Costas" online via YouTube.

MOVING FORWARD

We have established that getting scrappy can be a powerful, game-changing tool. But a scrappy *attitude* alone will get you only part of the way there. There are two other components to round out this concept: You have to be willing to build a scrappy *strategy* and then take action in order to reach your goal.

One last mention of *Apollo 13*: In the 1995 movie about that historic mission, Tom Hanks portrays Commander Jim Lovell. There's one scene early in the film that will always be my favorite: Hanks, as Lovell, is sitting beside his wife in their backyard, staring at the night sky shortly after *Apollo 11* has safely landed on the moon. He looks over at her and says, "We now live in a world where a man has walked on the moon. It's not a miracle. We just decided to go."

Now it's your turn to decide to go.

REVIEW

- How does deciding to go change the game? It works similarly to a railroad switch. Choosing to get scrappy is disruptive to your brain's normal pattern, and this disruption activates a shift in your mind that helps stimulate your creativity.
- The ideas don't come first, the commitment does. There's no specific time line for how long it will take for your brain to come up with a solution. It will happen when it happens.
- What happens if the stakes are high and you don't have a lot of time? Ultimately you have to do the best you can with what you have got.
- DARPA creates an atmosphere specifically suited to produce breakthroughs where leading minds are encouraged to embrace a model of learning balanced on three crucial elements:
  - Ambitious goal
  - Temporary project teams/finite time frame
  - Independence
- There are many similarities that parallel the conditions for getting scrappy with the elements of the DARPA model.
- When these conditions combine, we have an atmosphere in which a scrappy mindset thrives. That leads to a new way of viewing—and solving—the puzzle before you.

Chapter Activity: Whatever your goal is, you're not crazy to try, but you would be crazy to try without putting some thought into it. Let's put it all together.

1. Think about how you might start playing bigger in your life. Begin by identifying a goal you want to focus on and write it down.

   My goal is to:

   Share your goal with a mentor or trusted colleague. This high-level focus will help to align your senses. With total clarity of your mission comes a freedom to get as creative as possible and do everything you can to succeed—within professional and ethical boundaries.

2. Consider the people you might need/want on your team and establish a finite time line or goal date for your project if it doesn't already have one.

   Possible team members or support:

Time line/Goal date/Deadline date:

_____

_____

3. Do you have the freedom to take action? How will you build
   a favorable environment in order to reach your goal?

_____

_____

_____

_____

_____

_____

What's Next: In the next section we will begin to explore the
elements necessary to develop your strategy.

Part 2
STRATEGY

A scrappy strategy encompasses all of your efforts: research, due diligence, and sweat equity—and helps you channel them in the most productive direction. It's the tactical planning necessary to achieve a specific goal. This section is divided into three chapters that frame the prep work necessary before you can execute. Chapter 4 focuses on things to consider when developing your scrappy approach. Chapter 5 will discuss the investment you will need to make in the process to prepare for "game day." With a solid approach and the appropriate homework completed, you can then begin cultivating fresh ideas with chapter 6.

Chapter 4

DEVELOPING YOUR
SCRAPPY APPROACH

*Never give up on a dream just because of the time it will take
to accomplish it. The time will pass anyway. . . .*

—**Earl Nightingale**

SO YOU HAVE DECIDED TO GO AND ARE READY TO BEGIN THE
process of crafting a scrappy strategy. You are moving forward to a
different level, thinking less about the challenges and focusing
more on finding solutions.

At the end of the last chapter, you were asked to think about
setting a specific goal. Don't just check a box on your "things to do"
list; choose something that inspires you to play bigger. This is your
life, your dream. Get that big client or dream prospect to work with
you. Inspire the amazing mentor you have looked up to for years to
teach and counsel you in a particular field. Persuade the generous

individual you have been prospecting to donate a large sum of money to your philanthropic effort or cause. Run for an elected office to bring about the changes you have been fighting for. Take your business to a new level through partnerships. Go for that huge promotion. You get to choose, so why not play big? Imagine what it will be like when people say to you:

"How did you close that deal and land that client?"

"I can't believe you got Ms. Amazing to be your mentor! That's incredible."

"How in the world did you get the donor to write that check and support your cause?"

"Congratulations on taking your business public . . . receiving that big promotion . . . et cetera."

How did you do it? You chose to get scrappy!

Once you've defined your goal, the next step is to lay the groundwork for your scrappy approach. Whatever the goal is that you want to accomplish, there will be one or more decision makers who will be necessary to help you get there. Without their green light, it's only an idea in your head.

Ask yourself a few basic questions: Who is the decision maker you will need to contact? What kind of research can you do to find out how best to approach them? Do you need a quick solution, or are you working on the long game? What's your time frame? This chapter will help you to answer those questions, and the answers will shape your scrappy approach. Think of yourself as a pilot developing the flight plan that will ultimately take you to your final destination. There are options and alternate routes to consider. It takes time and research, but without it you could wander miles off course. It might not be the most enjoyable of tasks, but it is critical to your success.

To pull it all together, I will show you how to cultivate ideas, explore uncharted territory, do some homework, assess your timing, define the boundaries of your effort, and optimize the resources you have in hand—all in preparation for taking action. Remember, to earn the right to be heard you have to customize your approach in a way that is unrivaled. I'm talking about really rolling up your shirtsleeves and getting a little scrappy.

RESEARCHING THE RECIPIENT OF YOUR EFFORT

With your goal in mind, the next step will be to identify the person or people you need to impress in order to win their favor and achieve your goal. Who is the one person who has to say yes for you to move forward with your project? Is it the vice president of sales and marketing? An investor? An important buyer? Someone who can introduce you to a key person?

Once you have chosen your key person, ask yourself these three key questions:

1. What do I know about this individual or the people on this committee?
2. What might be a classy way to approach this person or group?

3. Have I ever met this person or is he a complete stranger? If he is a stranger, who do I know that might be able to introduce me or at least give me additional information about him?

Is it possible to gather some intel before you approach the decision maker you're meeting? This requires natural curiosity and active listening. Don't go for the typical kids and sports questions. Those don't impress or dazzle to win. Instead, ask your prospect about his or her favorite authors, bands, hobbies, and movies. Can't talk directly to a prospect? Get the information from their friend, colleague, or administrative assistant.

Use your imagination and think of something fun, interesting, and fresh. Through the years, I have done lots of crazy little things to employ scrappy efforts, including sending a prospect a Pets.com puppet I learned she really wanted so she would choose to work with me instead of one of my competitors; finding a special Disney menorah and sending it to my publisher to get him to meet with me to discuss giving my book more support; delivering organic cashews and green tea as a thank-you follow-up treat after a visit; obtaining signed books from a client's favorite author; special ordering a handmade vase from a young local artist; giving unique embroidered pillows to speakers that said SPEAKER OF THE HOUSE to thank them for sharing their time and pearls of wisdom with me; watching *The Bassmasters* and learning about bass fishing to connect with a difficult prospect; and even working free of charge to support someone else's effort in order to just get some face time to meet with them.

Here's a recent example of a small, scrappy, creative effort I utilized to stand out in the minds of a couple of powerful business-women I wanted to connect with in a more personal way:

I went to an event to see a gentleman from Mattel talk about the marketing and positioning of the international toy company. He highlighted the progress of some of their key product lines like Hot Wheels and Barbie. It was a great talk, and I particularly enjoyed the insight on the evolution of Barbie, including the launch of the new Entrepreneur Barbie within the Career Barbie line—love her! I grew up playing with the dolls, so of course I had to have one. Then I bought a couple of extra to support the idea of Entrepreneur Barbie and spread the word. I made a list of my hard-charging, scrappy entrepreneur business associates who I thought would appreciate her too and sent them the dolls as a little holiday treat.

They went crazy for her! This small gesture had my phone ringing, and it was so fun to see the reaction! These power women posted pictures of their new Barbies on Facebook, and almost all of them said they purchased additional dolls for their friends, daughters' friends, and more. Here's one of my favorite social media posts about the gift: "I just got this Christmas gift in the mail and could not LOVE it more. This is so me!!!"

This small gesture was such a hit, I bought a bunch more. Some of the women I sent Barbie to had children, some did not, but they all fell in love with Entrepreneur Barbie. I asked a couple of the ladies if they gave Barbie to their daughters and they said, "Um, no! She's mine!" and we laughed! It was a fun holiday season.

None of these ideas just popped into my head. I have invested a great deal of time and energy over the years in cultivating creative ideas that I trust to help me stay connected to others in a special way.

Each successful connection was the result of a bit of study and investigation because in the end, getting scrappy requires far more than just nerve and gumption. It requires you to research the recipients of your message, consider their interests and needs, and try to envision how you might pique their curiosity and earn their respect to obtain some of their time.

Determine the Best Timing of Your Approach

When you think about approaching the decision maker you want to connect with, where do you see a scrappy effort being most helpful? At what point along your journey will a scrappy effort have the most impact—in the beginning, in the middle, or as a follow-up near the end of the process? Are you trying to make a dazzling first impression? Is your project stalled in the middle of an opportunity and you want to create some movement to keep things progressing in a positive way? Or have you already made your best effort and just want to do something classy and clever to follow up with a specific decision maker or team? Timing will be a driving force behind the planning required to bring your scrappy effort to fruition. The following examples demonstrate the variables in timing your approach and will help you determine when your efforts will be most effective.

Before

Brian Palmer is an entrepreneur and the president of National Speakers Bureau, an agency that provides speakers and entertainment to corporations for meetings and conferences. (He might be the president, but he is also a salesperson for his company.) Brian had been diligently trying to win the business of a particular prospect—the executive vice president at a large financial services firm. Brian had made several attempts, but just couldn't get anything started and wanted to get his foot in the door. This prospect would reach out to Brian's company periodically for information, but never actually hired a speaker. Time to get scrappy.

Brian had previously worked with one of the company's meeting professionals, so he seized an opportunity to pick her brain about the executive he was trying to win over. "One day I asked her over the phone, 'Why is it that other parts of the company have become regular customers of mine yet I can't get anywhere with this guy?'" he recalled. The meeting professional was brutally honest, sharing a key piece of intel she had picked up from the executive earlier that same day. The executive said somewhat tongue in cheek, "Brian Palmer doesn't suck up enough!" And the executive was serious— he actually preferred a little sucking up when doing business.

That bit of information blindsided him because Brian is an authentic guy who doesn't believe in faking his way through a sale. He laughed at what he thought was a totally absurd situation. "Before I hung up the phone I asked, 'Does he have a good sense of humor?' and she said, 'Yes, absolutely.'"

Not one to let anyone spoil his day, Brian told me:

> *I took it in the best way I could—then I took a big risk, and did something that I knew he will never forget. After the call it dawned on me that at lunch that day I had gone to Target and bought a Black & Decker Dustbuster—and that's when the idea came to me. I went out to the car, grabbed my new, unopened Dustbuster, found a shipping box that I could put it in and*

included a note that said, "Dear David, Though I prefer to do my sucking up in person, please accept this gift for the times that I can't be there. Brian Palmer."

The package was a big hit. The elusive executive vice president went nuts when the box arrived—in a good way. Apparently he carried the Dustbuster around the senior executive area, showing it off to his coworkers and telling everyone about the humorous and thoughtful gift he'd received. "My business with him and a couple of other key people within the organization soared," Brian said. "A year later, I sent him a box of refills for that Dustbuster just to help keep the momentum going!"

Well played, Brian.

A brief note on gifts: It's all about giving and creating a favorable impression. It doesn't have to send you into debt. Nothing I have ever done has been expensive, just thoughtful and creative. We are not trying to buy their business. We are working to show people that we are authentically making an effort to connect with them and earn the right to be heard.

During

Sometimes you have to get scrappy in the middle of your journey. Things are moving along nicely, but you want to speed up the game, make things happen, and improve your circumstances in a challenging market. The story of my friend and entrepreneur Brandon Steiner illustrates just how vital maintaining a scrappy mindset can be to developing a successful long game over years, and even decades. Brandon is the owner of Steiner Sports Marketing & Memorabilia, which specializes in helping companies use the power of sports to grow their businesses. The company has spent more than twenty-five years building relationships and partnerships with athletes and national sports leagues. In his book *You Gotta Have Balls,* Brandon reveals how a lifelong fascination with quirky and obscure items ultimately led him to establish a multimillion-dollar sports memorabilia company.

> *I've always loved quirky sports memorabilia. For example, when the Colorado Avalanche won the Stanley Cup, I bought hockey pucks that had melted ice from the rink inside. Oddball things hit a nerve with me. . . . I'm always ready to go right up to the edge of the cliff when everybody's rolling their eyes and telling me not to jump. The more people don't see something, or don't agree with it, the more interesting it becomes to me—and, the more I enjoy the process of developing that market and activating it.*

In an interview, Brandon told me about the winding road he took—and the many stops and starts along the way—to build Steiner Sports.

> *So back in the 1990s when I was just starting to build the company, we were small. We didn't have money for a research and development department. We had me—hitting up malls, flea markets, street fairs, and Walmart for the latest craze in memorabilia. I love that stuff. I would keep it on my desk and stare at it. From time to time, it would help me trigger creative ideas. One*

day I started to think about old Yankee Stadium, about what a special place that was. So many great players—from Mickey Mantle to Joe DiMaggio to Derek Jeter—have walked on that field. There have been some pretty cool people walking on that dirt. I started thinking maybe, just maybe, people would be willing to buy a piece of that history.

One day I was looking at Derek Jeter out on the field, and I was just thinking, "I know I can sell his jersey, his hat. But it's very expensive and many people can't afford it. What can I do that will give people a little piece of one of baseball's most popular players?" And then, sure enough, I stopped staring at his jersey and his hat and looked underneath his feet, at the dirt. There was a lot of it. Slowly I began imagining not only a single product, but an entire product line centered around the appeal of owning a bit of authentic Yankee baseball history. I first pitched the idea to the Yankees in 2004 when we first started Yankees-Steiner Collectibles, and they were a little confused by my request to scoop dirt off the infield but they agreed. I think we started with little capsules full of dirt and we attached them to photos of all the best players. We also sprayed a little adhesive on the photos and sprinkled dirt on it to create a 3-D effect. And we were rolling!

Some people laughed, but I was dead serious. We made sure there was an authenticator there. We depended on authenticators to verify that the dirt actually came from Yankee Stadium. So we not only had somebody at the stadium pulling the dirt, we had our own people in our warehouse where we took the dirt and put it into the capsules. We began pairing dirt from specific areas on the field with the corresponding players. Customers seemed to love it.

About three to four years later, the economy started to skid and it became clear to Brandon that customers were looking to spend a lot less money on discretionary items. But he noticed that the company's dirt keepsakes, which were, on average, less expensive than anything else on his Web site, were doing well. So he branched out to other baseball stadiums and began selling dirt from Fenway Park and Wrigley Field and even dirt from specific games.

We had Home Run Derby dirt. We had All-Star Game dirt. Eventually, we went to all the teams in Major League Baseball and started getting dirt from all of them. And what's interesting is the viscosity and color of all the different dirt was really unique. So people actually started collecting the dirt from the different teams.

Sure, this was as you would say, an out-of-the-box idea, but ultimately it still took a lot of time to execute. Working with all of the different teams and stadiums took well over a year. But the good news was it started with one big idea—Yankee dirt, which was the crème de la crème. It took us about another year to get the dirt from all the other stadiums, possibly another eighteen months. But once we had the Yankee dirt, there was just a whole bunch of products that came out of that.

In fact, one of our most popular dirt collectibles evolved out of a thank-you gift I gave Brian Cashman, the general manager of the New York Yankees, who had done a lot of favors for me. I asked my designers to create a map of all the stadiums in the league, and they came and they showed me this map of the United States showing all the different stadiums. I said, "You know, we

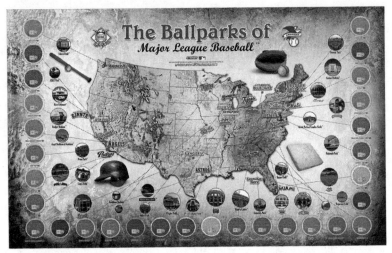

"The Ballparks of Major League Baseball"—Steiner Sports Memorabilia
(dirt map)

*have dirt from all those teams. Let's just put a capsule of dirt
underneath each stadium." They did and it looked great. When
I wrote my note to Brian, thanking him for everything he'd done,
I said, "Brian, now you have a little dirt on every team in your
office!" He loved it, so we made more. And sure enough, we've sold
thousands of those dirt maps of all different teams and players.*

Today at Steiner Sports, dirt is everywhere—dirt pins, dirt
clocks, dirt in bats! The company, which has seen more than $50
million in dirt sales, has even expanded into football and soccer
stadiums and golf courses.

*So it really has led to quite a bit of success, and I think a lot of it
started when our backs were against the wall in the recession when*

people really started cutting down on spending. What people forget is that sometimes the best idea is right underneath the one you already have. And instead of looking for the next best idea, sometimes the best move is just to extend the good idea you already have.

Brandon Steiner has been getting scrappy for years, and his story reveals a very layered and progressive strategy based on trial and error, a significant financial investment, and knowledge of the industry. You may not be ready for that, and that's okay. There's no reason to overwhelm yourself, especially if this is your first effort in getting scrappy. Your actions should be appropriate to the situation and your experience. Getting scrappy isn't always about making a grand gesture or putting forth a huge effort. Even though I have given you countless examples of big efforts that may have dazzled, small actions can have a big impact too. I want to point out here that I believe everyone should start small, but eventually you might want to go for a much bigger play. It's important to consider the range and scope of long- and short-term efforts.

After

Another occasion when you may want to employ a scrappy effort is after you have made your best effort. For example, you have delivered your best presentation to a client and you're waiting for a decision, or you have completed your final interview with a prospective company and you hope they will choose you over the other candidates. At this point, it might be nice to follow up in a memorable way to separate yourself from the competition. JD Cargill shares the following illustration:

I think it's important to stand out, and I certainly did my best to do so when applying for my job at CNN. It was my dream job, after all. I believe it was during our third or fourth interview with Karen, the woman who I would directly report to if hired, that our mutual love of orchids popped up. So when it came time to send my thank-you notes out to everyone I interviewed with, you can be damn sure hers included a beautiful, elegant white orchid.

When I did end up getting the job it turned out Karen's office was right next to mine and I had a direct view of her desk—where to my delight I saw a beautiful white orchid. I must have watched that flower bloom for the first six months I was on the job! Who knows what role it actually played, if any at all, in my hire, but all the same, every time I saw it I would smile. It represented something really powerful for me. I knew that I had done everything I could professionally to be qualified for the job, but for me that flower meant I had gone even further with a personal touch. As you would say, Terri, I got "scrappy"!

Granted, while on this scale of hire a small gesture like a thank-you plant likely has little weight, I couldn't help but hope that, in some small way, it might have helped. It's a very complicated and complex decision to hire an executive amongst several extremely qualified candidates—maybe the "orchid guy" stands out just a bit more. And even if it didn't help one bit, who cares! It enhanced my view for months!

A scrappy strategy can be helpful at varying points along your journey. For Brian Palmer, it was at the beginning of the process when he needed a trigger to help stimulate a relationship he was struggling to develop. Brandon Steiner morphed his plan repeatedly over time in order to adapt to a changing marketplace, whereas JD Cargill took action as a follow-up after a meeting to leave a memorable impression. Different scenarios call for different strategies, so remember to stay nimble and open to modifications as circumstances change.

KEEP THE LONG GAME IN MIND

You may be looking for a quick solution right now, but it's important to keep the "long game" in mind as well. It may require several ideas, multiple approaches, and more time than you originally anticipated (before, during, and after you connect with a decision maker) before you see anything happen. Stephanie Melish, a young businesswoman, had a very specific goal to change her career path and move into education and consulting. She had found an exciting opportunity with a training company that she really wanted. She was introduced to the perfect mentor who saw her potential, and after an exploratory interview with the company she was hooked. Unfortunately, Stephanie was told that while they were interested in her, they were not yet in a place to hire her.

> *I could have let "the timing isn't right" stop me . . . [but] I wasn't about to let it slip away. . . . I followed up with a handwritten thank-you, a predictable action that anyone could and probably would do. I knew it wouldn't suffice. If I wanted a job that*

did not exist, I needed to do the unpredictable; I needed to make an unforgettable impression. So I launched my full-on, balls-to-the-wall, you're-going-to-hire-me-no-matter-what campaign.

Stephanie was all in and focused her energy to build a strategy that would impress the key decision maker. "I found creative ways to deliver my message and stay connected. I refused to be forgotten." She subscribed to anything and everything related to the business, read everything ever written by her mentor, filmed herself presenting the material, and burned it to a CD and mailed it as a follow-up. She also e-mailed updates about her mindset, goals, ambitions, dreams, and more.

Several months later and a few short replies from his assistant thanking me, there was still no job offer. I was feeling deflated and defeated. Doubt had set in. Was it time to give up?

Hell no! I determined. If I wanted to know if I was going to get the job, I needed to make a formal effort and ask for it. [This man is known for his aggressive, outspoken style and personality, so I thought maybe it was time to make a bold move.] Some may call me crazy, but at one of my potential boss's seminars, in a room with eight hundred people during the Q&A session, I took a leap of faith and asked . . . "Are you going to hire me?" And from the stage he said calmly, "Yes." In the end it was that simple. I stayed the course, I put in the effort, I asked for the job, and I got it.

Stephanie's consistent scrappy efforts and tenacious approach worked cumulatively over the span of eight months to help her reach her goal. As the old saying goes, sometimes slow and steady wins the race. Stephanie believes, "You can wait and be forgotten or you can act and be remembered. Either way, the time is going to pass."

As you move forward into the next phase of developing your approach, keep in mind the importance of identifying the appropriate recipient of your effort, consider the best time to deploy your scrappy strategy, and keep the long game in mind.

REVIEW

- The first step when developing your scrappy strategy is to identify key decision makers who will be necessary to help you get where you want to go. Without their green light, it's only an idea in your head.
- Determine the best timing of your approach. Will it be most helpful at the beginning, in the middle, or at the end of the process? *When* you choose to engage the decision maker depends on where you are in the process.

Chapter Activity: At the end of the last chapter, you were asked to begin thinking about setting a specific goal. What did you choose? Did you modify your goal to make a bigger play after reading this chapter?

Who is the decision maker you will need to contact?

What kind of research can you do to execute effectively?

Do you need a quick solution, or are you working on the long game?

When will you launch your approach? Before, during, or after?

There are options and alternate routes to consider. It takes time and research, but without it you could wander miles off course. Get some of your ideas down on paper. It might not be the most enjoyable of tasks, but it is critical to your success.

What's Next: The next step on the path to discovering your best scrappy approach is investing in the process of exploration and preparation—in other words, doing the research you need to do so that you can be one step ahead of your competition!

Getting in the Ring—Bonus Scrappy Success Story #2

WHAT'S THE BEST TIMING TO MAKE A REQUEST OF THE DALAI LAMA?

SOMETIMES, IN THE PROCESS OF GETTING SCRAPPY, YOU COME up with a really wild, over-the-top idea. Some people might even think you're crazy. Roman Tsunder, the cofounder and CEO of PTTOW!, an invite-only marketing summit, knows a thing or two about this. His annual conference—which often is referred to as the TED of the marketing world—brings together media magnates, artists, cultural icons, and business leaders to discuss innovation.

In 2013, Roman, who also founded Access 360 Media, was looking to create an unbelievable event for the attendees of his annual PTTOW! Summit. Around the same time, he had become friendly with Lama Tenzin, the Dalai Lama's emissary for peace. Roman said, "I had this impossible idea . . . I'm going to see if the Dalai Lama wants to come to PTTOW!" This was a bold idea and would not be an easy task. In addition, it is considered inappropriate to make a direct request of a monk in regard to the Dalai Lama. Roman had to carefully raise the idea at lunch with Lama Tenzin during a discussion about young people and their role in the world. Lama Tenzin didn't say no. In fact, he agreed to meditate on the idea and speak to His Holiness about it.

Three months later—well past the time he should be settling on a speaker—Roman had another conversation with Lama Tenzin about the conference and was told the Dalai Lama was terribly busy. Roman figured it was over and thought it was stupid to even consider such a feat. But then Lama Tenzin cheerfully added that "the elders are meditating on it." Roman wasn't sure what that meant but he figured it couldn't hurt and trusted that it was a good sign.

By January, he still hadn't heard anything and was pretty much ready to give up. Then he received a call from Lama Tenzin and the conversation eventually wound its way around to PTTOW! Lama Tenzin told Roman that the Dalai Lama thought "what you're doing is a good thing." Roman was beside himself, overjoyed simply to have been acknowledged by the Dalai Lama. He thanked Lama Tenzin profusely and then decided to mention PTTOW! *one more time* in a carefully worded question that wasn't quite a direct request. "So I said, 'Since we are three months away from this event, do you think that it makes sense that we reserve a hotel room to make sure the Dalai Lama is comfortable?'" Roman recalled. "And Lama Tenzin said, 'Yes, yes, yes. That is a good idea. He will join you.'"

Roman was definitely playing big. He had to carefully respect the cultural customs and manage the timing of his approach (before, during, *and* as a follow-up) to the decision makers about his request. You might find yourself in a similar position. Timing and respecting the nuances of the situation are critical to executing an effective scrappy effort.

Chapter 5

INVESTING IN THE PROCESS

AT THIS POINT, YOUR GOAL IS BEFORE YOU. YOU HAVE CON-
sidered the best timing of your approach and identified the decision
makers you want to connect with. The next step on the path to developing your best scrappy strategy is to do the prep work necessary
to stay ahead of your competition. You will want to do your research
and perform your due diligence. It's vital to crafting the plan that
will move you closer to where you want to be.

People, especially those in charge, rarely invite you into their
offices and give freely of their time. Instead, you have to do something unique, compelling, even funny or a bit daring, to earn it. Even
if you happen to be an exceptionally well-rounded person who possesses all of the scrappy qualities discussed so far, it's still important
to be prepared, dig deep, do the prep work, and think on your feet.

Harry Gordon Selfridge, who founded the London-based

department store Selfridges, knew the value of doing his homework. Selfridge, an American from Chicago, traveled to London in 1906 with the hope of building his "dream store." He did just that in 1909, and more than a century later, his stores continue to serve customers in London, Manchester, and Birmingham. Selfridges' success and staying power is rooted in the scrappy efforts of Harry Selfridge himself, a creative marketer who exhibited "a revolutionary understanding of publicity and the theatre of retail," as he is described on the Selfridges' Web site. His department store was known for creating events to attract special clientele, engaging shoppers in a way other retailers had never done before, catering to the holidays, adapting to cultural trends, and changing with the times and political movements such as the suffragists.

Selfridge was noted to have said, "People will sit up and take notice of you if you will sit up and take notice of what makes them sit up and take notice."

How do you get people to take notice? How do you stand out in a positive way in order to make things happen? The curiosity and imagination Selfridge employed to successfully build his retail stores can be just as valuable for you to embrace in your circumstances. Perhaps you have landed a meeting, interview, or a quick coffee date with a key decision maker at a company that has sparked your interest. To maximize the impression you're going to make, you have to know your audience. That means you must respectfully learn what you can about the person, their industry, or the culture of their organization. In fact, it pays to become familiar not only with the person's current position but also their background, philosophies, triumphs, failures, and major breakthroughs. With that information in hand, you are less likely to waste the precious time you have and more likely to engage in genuine and meaningful conversation.

This chapter is about gathering the information you need to devise the most effective tactics for your strategy. Think of this phase as the staging area where you will line up the tools and hone the talents needed to complete your effort. You will explore the value of doing your homework, expanding your network, developing your personal skill set, spending a little money, and working with a mentor or adviser. As with most meaningful tasks, the more research and homework you do, the more confident you will feel about moving forward.

TRAINING AND PREPARATION BEFORE YOU "GET INTO THE RING"

From a tactical perspective, it is unrealistic to think that you are going to magically come up with a truly clever plan without putting some time, energy, and effort into "training for the fight." A boxer may have a scrappy attitude, but she had better put her time in at the gym with a solid coach and learn about her opponent before stepping into the ring with a fierce competitor.

Retired American professional boxer Laila Amaria Ali is the daughter of the legendary retired heavyweight boxer Muhammad Ali. She is considered one of the top ten female boxers of all time—and she is a scrapper! As the undefeated super middleweight champion of our generation, she definitely knows a thing or two about training and preparing before you get in the ring.

In her book *Reach!: Finding Strength, Spirit, and Personal Power*, Ali shares her story as an example of someone willing to reach beyond circumstances they don't like. Her commitment to training and preparing for each fight directly relates to the principles of preparation when getting scrappy. Laila says, "Being unafraid and aggressive isn't enough; mastering the skills is what makes a fighter complete."

Ali was born with natural talent, but when going up against a competitor like Kendra Lenhart, "a 6-foot-2 veteran with a reputation as an especially hard hitter," she says it forced her "to use strategy, not just punching power."

She reminds us that there will be wins and losses along the way. Training is about minimizing losses and increasing wins through preparation. The goal is not just to wildly throw punches, but to be conscious, aware, and throw punches that land beautifully.

So how can you kick your scrappy training into a higher gear before stepping into the ring? The objective right now is to further develop your knowledge and skill set and design a solid foundation to build from—a new set point of perspective. Insight, skill, and timing—all of these elements will make you a more formidable competitor and awaken the interest of a decision maker in your proposition.

You want to cultivate a connection, spark interest, and show you are unique, so go above and beyond what the general public will do and learn as much as you can within the time allotted to stand out and play bigger! Some efforts require just a little bit of homework while others will require much more. It's a case-by-case basis. I recommend any or all of the following simple methods of tackling homework for a scrappy effort:

1. Search the Internet
2. Expand your network
3. Develop your personal skill set
4. Invest a bit of money
5. Work with a mentor

Search the Internet

Motivational "sales intelligence" speaker Sam Richter believes in doing his homework before meeting with someone new. He calls it his "3x5 Rule" and applies it to every aspect of his business. "Never ever, ever, ever meet with somebody without spending three minutes trying to find five pieces of information, or five minutes trying to find three pieces of information. That's it. It's not that hard."

To help gather those details, Richter uses online tools including LinkedIn and YouGotTheNews.com, a Web site that culls the nation's newspapers for personal tidbits. "And it could be from large newspapers, it could be from the *Poughkeepsie Weekly News*," Richter says. "Because that's where people are covered. That's where a wedding announcement's going to be." Sam's Internet strategy for doing your homework is about truly creating an authentic human connection. The goal, he says, is to locate a piece of information that will give you permission to ask a great question. "And what's beautiful is that with today's mobile devices, you can do that in a car just before a meeting. If you've got a job interview, just take out your smart phone while you're sitting in the lobby. It's easy to do; you just have to think about it."

One of Sam's favorite homework success stories is from back in 2011 when he took his own advice and applied his 3x5 Rule to learn about an executive named Laurin McCracken, whom he was hoping to get a contract with for a pending project: "So I'm sitting in my rental car and I do the 3x5. I Google Laurin McCracken and I soon find out that it's a Mr. Laurin McCracken. (Because that would not be scrappy if I walked in and asked for Mrs. McCracken. . . .)"

Sam discovered that McCracken was a world-class watercolor painter and even perused his Web site. During their lunch together, Sam brought it up in conversation.

> *"Hey, Laurin, I really appreciate you seeing me today. As you may know, before I meet with people . . . I do my homework. I did a little bit of Google research on you and guess what I found? I found your Web site about watercolor painting and I'm fascinated. How does one become a world-class watercolor painter?"*
>
> *Now, here's the key to being scrappy . . . you've got to be genuine. If I was using that technique because I wanted to "manipulate" Laurin it wouldn't work because smart people know when they're being manipulated. But I was genuinely and authentically interested. I looked at his work and at first I thought it was photography, it was so darn good. So what did we talk about for the first forty-five minutes of our lunch? We talked about Laurin and his watercolor work.*

I asked Sam, "How did you segue back into your professional conversation? You have done your homework, you're in the meeting, and you get to reference the fact that it's a genuine interest. How do you segue from talking about watercolors to getting into the heart and soul of your visit?" Sam replied:

More often than not, the other person will bring it up . . . It might sound something like, "Oh Sam, I feel so bad. I spent the first twenty minutes talking about me. Gosh, you came all the way to Dallas. Tell me a little about you and how you can help us." . . . And that's a segue.

In a case where they don't initiate the transition (which also happens), I might say something like . . . "I would love to continue to talk about this but I respect your time and I want to make sure we take care of what we came here to do today so . . ."

Here's another scrappy idea tying back to the same story and the value of using the Internet, but relating to follow-up after your meeting or visit. Sam suggests,

Never follow up with a boring thank-you note. I try to align my thank-you note with a piece of information I've gathered in the meeting or conversation that is important to the other person. During my visit with Laurin McCracken, he shared that he would be giving the keynote address at the 2011 Chinese Watercolor Conference. I said, "What's wrong with that?"

He said, "I don't know anything about Chinese watercolors. I'm terrified."

This was the nugget I needed to do a little more research . . . I found online the keynote address from the 2010 Chinese Watercolor Conference. So in my thank-you note I said, "Hey, Laurin, so nice to meet with you. I really hope to have the opportunity to work with you and Jacobs Engineering sometime in the future." And the next paragraph said, "By the way, I stumbled across this online." (Of course, I didn't just stumble on it.) "It is the keynote address from the 2010 Chinese Watercolor Conference and I thought it might be helpful to you as you prepare your speech for the conference." (Talk about differentiating yourself just in the thank-you note. . . .)

I asked Laurin once we had become friends, "You know, I sent you that thank-you note with the keynote address information. . . . Did you think it was any good?"

He said, "Sam, not only was it good"—and these were his exact words, I'll remember it forever— "you're one of the first people I've ever met with who genuinely cared, genuinely took the time to care."

Sam's story shows the value of remembering that preparing for an interview or researching a decision maker ahead of a key meeting is about more than just digging for information. It's an opportunity to explore someone else's personal and professional achievements in an authentic and classy way.

Expand Your Network

Forging connections with others is one of the most basic, yet valuable tools in reaching your goal. Expand your circle of influence. Identify colleagues, experts, and friends who can help you line up referrals and elegant introductions to key players in the industry or company you're hoping to work with. Networking is all about initiating conversations and engaging with people who can provide specific insight and incredible data in a way that you can't read about in a book or online. It's always great to make new friends and to develop

relationships with others who are deeply interested in similar sub-
jects. That mutual interest you share will stimulate your mind and,
quite frankly, it's fun.

Your network will help you to expand your reach significantly. I
didn't know all of the people in this book before I sat down to really
write it. I tapped into my network with a very specific intention to
connect with and learn about more scrappy people—men and
women with great stories who were beyond my contact database.
Writing this book was absolutely an exercise in putting forth scrappy
effort to cultivate the content. Sometimes I got the meeting, thanks
to my network . . . and sometimes I didn't. Some of the meetings I
was able to secure will actually not happen until after this book is
complete, but I still want the visit. Who knows where those opportunities might lead?

I had to jump through some pretty crazy hoops to access a few
individuals—and then, even when I did, I couldn't always get the
interview or the information I wanted. But I still had fun trying,
learned some lessons, and it was great brain candy. For me, it's all
good, all just part of the journey.

Develop Your Personal Skill Set

An essential piece of developing a successful scrappy strategy is hon-
ing your talents and skills in preparation for game day. Such focused
preparation will mean different things to different people. To a college basketball player eager to improve his free-throw percentage, it
might mean sinking two hundred baskets a day for four weeks. For
a software sales executive looking to land a new client, it could mean
improving her presentation skills and upgrading her wardrobe.

As you explore and prepare for your goal, you may discover that additional requirements beyond your current skill set are important to a decision maker in a way you hadn't planned for. Here's an example on a small scale: At my company, we write lots of handwritten notes, and I need people on my team with decent penmanship. During the interview process we request that they submit a handwriting sample—certainly a skill that can be improved with practice. There was a very sweet young man who applied for an internship position with my company, and after his interview he made a point of delivering a handwritten note, which was great. His penmanship, however, looked like chicken scratch and was difficult to read. I couldn't figure out several of the words, so while I appreciated the effort, it wasn't an impressive execution.

What if you're pressed for time and you don't have three years to master a key skill required for a specific position you desire? Time to get scrappy!

A friend of mine, Josh Kaufman, explores this idea in greater depth in his book *The First 20 Hours: How to Learn Anything . . . Fast.* His whole premise is that there is a systematic approach to rapid learning acquisition. Josh says the keys are:

1. Decide exactly what you want to be able to do. What does useful performance really look like? (You don't have to be the best in the world to get useful results.)
2. Deconstruct the skill into the smallest possible subskills. Most skills are actually bundles or combinations of much smaller skills, so learn the fundamentals first.

3. Learn enough about each subskill to be able to practice intelligently and self-correct during practice. You don't have to learn everything there is to know, just enough to notice when you're making a mistake, then fix it.

4. Remove physical, mental, and emotional barriers that get in the way of practice. Make it as easy as possible to avoid distractions, maintain focused attention, and practice for 30–40 minutes without interruption.

5. Precommit to at least twenty hours of practice. Practicing the most important subskills first will make your practice more efficient, and twenty hours of practice is enough to see major results.

Inventory those skills you're going to need to execute your scrappy strategy and start doing the prep work, one day at a time. Be honest about your abilities. Investing in yourself is not only about mastering the things you do well, it's also about working on the things you don't do so well because you have to keep the long game in mind.

Spend a Bit of Money

Investing a bit of treasure in your scrappy strategy only makes sense. Perhaps you buy a plane ticket to attend a key trade show, hoping to meet new industry contacts. Maybe it means buying a new suit and splurging on an upscale haircut to truly "dress to impress" at your next appointment. Maybe it's sending a plant to the executive assistant who helped you get in the door. Or maybe it's hiring an outside service to support you in putting together a big play. Consider the following example from the Winspire organization:

A sales team for a global fuel company was working toward renewing a multimillion-dollar contract with a high-end client. They had made the presentation and were awaiting the final decision, but wanted to gain an edge over their competitors. The team members knew they needed to pull out all the stops and really dazzle the client in order to keep the business, so they hired Winspire to help them generate ideas about how to woo the company's CEO. (Winspire is a third-party vendor that provides highly sought-after, hard-to-find, unique experiences for use in charity auctions, special events, and corporate incentive programs.) After a great deal of research and a discussion with the internal staff, Winspire discovered that the CEO was a passionate golfer. So the sales team went to work researching additional information that might help them impress the CEO. They even contacted his private club, spoke with the club professional about the gentleman, and discovered that one of his lifelong dreams was to play a round of golf at Augusta National in Georgia—where the Masters is played.

That was the kind of intel they were looking for! The fuel company sales team knew if they could get the CEO onto that course, they would more than stand out from the rest of the field. The next challenge: how to make it happen? If you're not a golf fan, let me explain: Unless you know someone on the Augusta National Golf Club membership list, it's almost impossible to play there; even the pros need to win a PGA Tour event to get an invitation.

Time to get scrappy! So the fuel company made the decision to be all in, working with Winspire to find a friend, colleague, or associate who was a member of Augusta National with similar interests as the CEO and willing to set up a golf date. You cannot buy your way onto this course, so getting invited by a member was the only way they could make it happen.

According to Jeff Weber, executive vice president at Winspire, his team spent a considerable amount of time working the phones and reaching out to their connections in order to secure a round of golf for their client on the country's most exclusive and traditional course. "We worked our tails off to get to these guys on the Augusta National."

In the end, their scrappy efforts paid off. They succeeded in helping the fuel company gain access by using appropriate channels and still following the rules through the power of networking. (They found an associate who was genuinely interested in playing golf with the CEO and, fortunately, also a member of Augusta National.) The CEO was so pleased with the global fuel company's sales team, their efforts, and the additional conversations that took place on the course that he gave them his business and renewed the contract.

Was it worth it to hire an outside party to help generate ideas? In this case, absolutely. The global fuel company was so thrilled with the outcome that it began awarding all of its client entertainment business back to Winspire. In every way, the deal was a win-win-win, benefiting each entity on a long-term basis.

Work with a Mentor

Another great place to start when developing your talent is with a mentor. Mentors are people who have been where you want to go, and they are wonderful sounding boards for new ideas. They have experienced what you are trying to learn, and they know the pitfalls. If you are clever enough, you could probably figure out on your own much of what a mentor can teach you. But how long would it take? How much energy would you expend? You might get there eventually, but why go through that taxing process when someone already knows the answers to your questions?

Since the early days of my career, I have sought out mentors to help me at varying stages of my life. One of my first mentors in the speaking industry was Floyd Wickman. In 1996, we actually coauthored a book called *Mentoring: A Success Guide for Mentors and Protégés*. Floyd wrote from the perspective of "how to be a mentor" while I wrote from the viewpoint of the protégé. The book is now out of print and a lot has changed since it was first published, but I recently had the opportunity to revisit the material with Floyd and we talked about how even though much has changed, some things have stayed the same. Here are some of our key takeaways:

- The most successful mentoring relationships are protégé- (or mentee-) driven. The relationship succeeds when the protégé does the significant work and makes it happen. The mentor is the guide.
- Many mentors become protégés later in life as they launch second and even third careers.
- Age simply isn't a factor in terms of who plays which role.
- It's about the transfer of knowledge.
- Mentoring is a contact sport. The magic is in the connection— that mashup of trust, skepticism, brainstorming, push-back, laughter, and tears.

■ While countless studies have proven mentoring creates successful outcomes for both mentor and protégé, the best evidence is that which has not and cannot be scientifically measured—only shared through the stories of those who can testify how these relationships have dramatically changed their lives for the better.

Mentoring can be accomplished in a number of ways. Protégés can certainly take an active role in choosing a mentor by seeking out a specific person who has mastered a skill or craft they admire. But sometimes the most amazing mentor is found by happenstance. He or she shows up when the protégé is already on their path. Think about it—Luke Skywalker in *Star Wars* didn't walk around muttering, "OMG, if I only had Yoda!" But where would Luke Skywalker be without the wisdom and insight of Yoda on how to use the Force? Mr. Miyagi in the film *The Karate Kid* wasn't really looking for Daniel-san to take under his wing as a protégé, but where would Daniel be without Miyagi's guidance? And of course who could forget the scrappy fighting move, the Crane, which ultimately saved Daniel in the final fight that changed everything? Somehow they all found each other, and the mentoring relationship unfolded in a natural, organic way. Mentoring helps provide critical support, a sense of wisdom, and guidance on everything from timing to protocol. Mentors can show you how to execute from a more mature and informed dynamic that can be the "special sauce" in executing an effective effort.

This chapter has been all about investing in the process of exploration and preparation by doing the research necessary to be one step ahead of your competition. A scrappy fighter has to be "light" on her feet, agile, and sometimes quick to respond. You want to have a clear head, stay calm, be aware of your circumstances, and be ready for game day or a random big-play scenario. You just never know what small window of opportunity could open. A scrappy person is prepped and ready to respond in a winning fashion.

Get in the game! What do the best of the best do? How do they execute and win? How can you position yourself differently from what they do in order to beat them? It can be very helpful to know who your competition is and what they do if you want to craft a strategy to "slide right by . . . and get the win." With the right homework and preparation, they will never see you coming!

REVIEW

- Even if you happen to a be an exceptionally well-rounded person who possesses all of the scrappy qualities discussed so far, it's still important to be prepared, dig deep, do the prep work, and think on your feet before you get in the ring. Doing so will help you to eliminate fatigue and throw punches that land beautifully!
- Some efforts require just a little bit of homework while others will require much more. It's a case-by-case basis. I recommend any or all of the following simple methods of tackling homework for a scrappy effort:
  - Search the Internet
  - Expand your network
  - Develop your personal skill set

- Invest a bit of money
- Work with a mentor
- Be agile and quick to respond
- Get in the ring and go a few rounds. Watch and learn from others in your space. What do the best of the best do? How do they execute and win? Explore how you can position yourself differently from what they do. With the right homework and preparation, they will never see you coming!

Chapter Activity: Let's do some prep work. With your goal and a specific decision maker in mind, begin putting forth the effort to take action on the prep work below.

Search the Internet: Do what Sam suggested—employ the 3x5 Rule. Spend three minutes trying to find five pieces of information, or five minutes trying to find three pieces of information, on the person you're intending to connect or meet with and see what you can come up with.

Expand your network: Pick up the phone and reach out to a colleague or friend who can help you line up referrals and elegant introductions to key players in the industry or a company you're hoping to work with.

Develop your personal skill set: Choose one skill you want or need to improve upon and commit to at least twenty hours of practice. Take an online course, sign up to attend a live classroom event, work with a coach, and take action to expand your personal skill set.

Spend a bit of money on an important project (your goal): Sometimes you have to spend a little money or invest some sweat equity! Is it time for an upgrade to your résumé, or your professional look or attire? Is it time to take a chance on a big effort to dazzle a prospect? Choose one thing and make the investment.

Work with a mentor: Choose and seek out a specific person who has mastered a skill or craft that you admire. Make the effort to set up a call, meeting, or visit with them to obtain guidance on taking a well-thought-out "next step" to accomplish your goal.

What's Next: Now that you have done your homework and invested the time to better understand the interests and needs of your prospect or the decision makers on your journey, it's time to cultivate some specific tactical ideas. The next chapter will explore a variety of options—small, medium, and large.

Getting in the Ring—Bonus Scrappy Success Story #3

ARE YOU WILLING TO WORK FOR FREE IN HOPES OF GAINING AN OPPORTUNITY?

ABOUT FIVE OR SIX YEARS INTO HER CAREER, CHRISTINE Hassler, an author and a leading expert on Millennials, had the opportunity to interview with a big PR firm to become the spokeswoman for one of their major commercial brands. Hassler was beyond excited and wanted the role for many reasons: "The brand was amazing . . . I love doing TV . . . and being a spokesperson was something I hadn't done before," she says. "And, to be honest, it was a nice paycheck." The interview took place over the phone, involved countless questions, and went very smoothly. Hassler was hopeful.

About a week later, she got a call from the PR firm informing her that she was in the running but the client was leaning toward someone with a larger platform who was more well known. The company said it would make its final decision after sending out a survey to thousands of Millennials. The plan was to use the survey results to shape the upcoming campaign. Hassler immediately went on alert, asked a few questions, and discovered that the people who wrote the survey were in their forties. (Nothing against Gen Xers, but a Millennial might have some unique insight to provide when crafting the right questions to ask of their generation.) Though she knew the company might not hire her, she felt strongly that she could be of service and offered to take a look at the survey for free.

A day or two later, the PR firm took her up on her offer. After a quick look, she knew she could improve it, so she sat down and virtually rewrote the entire survey and sent it back. The PR firm and its client loved her work, hired her to be the spokeswoman, and flew her in for multiple speaking engagements. All in all, that one scrappy move generated five years of rewarding and lucrative business.

Chapter 6

CULTIVATING SCRAPPY IDEAS

I think scrappy people demonstrate intellectual curiosity through action. They anticipate, think, and amend. I love scrappy people!

—Roy Freiman, a vice president of strategy and analytics,
Prudential Financial

AS YOU START TO THINK ABOUT HOW TO DAZZLE A KEY decision maker, keep in mind that your options are virtually endless. You might feel more comfortable with a simple, classy approach at first. Or maybe you are thinking about doing something really big, amazing, and over-the-top. To earn the attention of a listener and create an opportunity for yourself in the process, the recipient must be pleasantly surprised in a positive way. Whatever idea you decide to run with, keep in mind that in order for your plan to work, the recipient of your gesture must *like it*. It doesn't matter if you would like it. What matters is whether or not he or she will like it.

Nicole and Pattie are two of my best friends—they love horror films, haunted house adventures, and visiting the Knott's Scary Farm amusement park at Halloween, where hundreds of monsters and ghouls jump out with the sole purpose of scaring the heck out of you. I hate scary movies and I have been to Knott's Scary Farm—let's just say I have absolutely no interest in ever going again. If my friends bought me a ticket to join them for a scary movie or to go to Knott's at Halloween, I would feel like I was being punished. If I bought them tickets, on the other hand, they would be ecstatic.

My mom loves marzipan chocolates, but I don't. When my dad gives my mom marzipan chocolates every year at Christmas, she is just as excited as she can be. If he gave me the same gift, I wouldn't be happy. I would say, "Gross, Dad, I can't believe you got me marzipan!"

The point is, it's important to customize your effort in a way that makes the receiver happy. It's not about what *you* want. It doesn't have to make sense to everyone, just you and the recipient of your effort. As you do your homework you will begin tinkering with a bunch of intel and data like ingredients in a stew—mixing, layering, tweaking, and morphing the recipe to craft your concept and approach based on what you know. The quest for great ideas is challenging, but also a fun adventure! In this chapter we will share specific, tactical ideas customized to meet the preferences of the receiver. We will explore a variety of options—small, medium, and large.

THINK THROUGH A VARIETY OF OPTIONS: SMALL, MEDIUM, OR LARGE

As you move forward, evaluate whether your effort is going to be before, during, or toward the end of your process, as well as small, medium, or large in scale. Sometimes your idea or solution to a problem is a simple, easy-to-execute effort. Small actions can have a big impact too. But again, sometimes the big ideas get the big results. Don't overcomplicate it if you don't have to! To help you begin developing your next strategy, here's a list of twenty-one unique ideas that others have used effectively. I provide these to help jumpstart your creativity, not as an exact plan for you to follow.

21 Scrappy Ideas People Have Used to Move Their Intentions Forward

Small Efforts

1. Handwrite personal cards and notes.

    Sending a good old-fashioned handwritten note is considered a rarity today. They rarely even teach cursive writing in classrooms anymore. Don't send generic holiday cards with custom engraving and no personal sentiment or note—that's just checking the box and doesn't make any impression at all, except to say, "You are one in a large stack of people on my holiday card list." So boring! You don't have to write a novel, just a line or two with a nice hello and your real signature.

2. Perform a random act of kindness.

A simple, polite gesture or a random act of kindness goes a long way. Someone whose attention you have been trying to capture may acknowledge and remember your effort. Brian Palmer has a touching story about a scrappy act of kindness that illustrates just how powerful this tool can be. He had a friend who contracted a serious illness and was in the hospital. "I knew it was going to be a long haul," he said. "And after a few days, I called up an excellent local Chicago pizza joint. I asked if they delivered to this hospital and they said yes." He ordered several pizzas and salad and had them write a personal greeting and thank-you to the medical professionals taking care of his friend on the lid of the pizza boxes. The food was a huge hit, his friend was deeply touched, and the nurses caring for her were appreciative as well. Later on she told Palmer his gesture made a noticeable difference in how the staff treated her and brightened a very dark time in her life.

3. Book a phone, coffee, or wine visit.

A simple phone call to someone can lead to a nice visit, even if it's not in person. Set it up in a way that is sincere and appealing. A missed opportunity to get together with a colleague for a glass of wine can turn into a long-distance wine chat. For example: A business associate of mine and I had a plan to meet up, but due to travel complications, we were unable to get together. One evening, she was in one hotel room across the country and I was in another. Neither one of us had anything to do, so we both ordered a glass of our favorite wine and had a great catch-up by phone.

If you are not as friendly with an individual, why not send a Starbucks card with an invitation and say: "Hey, want to meet for coffee? I know we're thousands of miles apart, but we can pretend we're together in person. Latte is on me!"

4. Start setting up meetings with big fish and people of influence to inspire future goal setting.

Why not try to schedule as many big-fish meetings with people of influence as possible and set yourself up to learn about how to do things in the future? The fastest way to get where you want to go is to learn how to navigate the best path from those who are currently successful doing what you want to do.

5. Include small tokens of gratitude.

I prefer to send a little gift along with thank-you notes— typically something small and simple. It makes getting the thank-you note a little more fun for the recipient. Examples: custom-made all-natural chocolates, organic cookies, books, whatever is best for the situation and the person I am thanking.

6. Reach out to people on the more unique holidays.

Instead of following the crowd and blending in with the masses by sending a traditional Christmas/Hanukkah/Kwanzaa/Season's Greetings card, why not skip that season altogether? I'm a big fan of sending Thanksgiving cards. You're thanking people for their business and friendship, and of course standing out from the crowd with a more unique and personal holiday wish. How about Happy New Year or St. Patrick's Day instead?

7. Deliver a message of "good luck" to someone who is working on a project.

They will remember your kind gesture. Include a small good-luck charm like a four-leaf clover or a small horseshoe to encourage their efforts and send positive wishes.

8. Customized small gestures can make a big impression.

I have a client who is an avid coin collector, and while I wouldn't be so presumptuous as to buy him a coin to add to his collection, I did make an extra effort to acquire an "Irish Claddagh Hands Friendship Pocket Token" coin, which I gave him as a thank-you following a project together. He was genuinely appreciative of the gesture and noted that small gestures can make a big impression.

9. Just do a clever little follow-up.

Do something memorable to revisit your contact after an appointment or meeting to stay "top of mind" with a key decision maker. Here's an example from my friend George Walther.

Small Example: The Wooden Spoon Story

I recall my early contacts with Nightingale-Conant Corporation, the world's largest publisher of nonmusic audio programs (at the time). I wanted to author a program for them. I'd made my proposal, things seemed to have gone well, I was eager to move ahead, and I could see no reason to delay. Looking back, I confess I was a bit overzealous and applied too much pressure in suggesting an immediate in-person visit to solidify the deal, but that's where my head was at the time.

My contact, Nick Carter, said: "Slow down, now. Let me tell you how things work around here. We've got a big stove down the hall with several kettles simmering on it. When we start considering a new program, we put the idea in a kettle and let it kind of simmer for a while (metaphorically speaking). Each time we pass the stove, we give the kettles a sniff. If they start to smell like money, we move ahead. But it's a slow process and you really can't rush us. If you want to call in a couple of weeks, I'll let you know if anything has changed."

I felt pretty sure that this was a brush-off, but jotted the date in my calendar anyway. Producing the program meant a lot to me and I knew I could do a great job for this publisher. I was determined to make it happen. I headed off to one of those import stores that carries lots of candles, cooking tools, and rattan furniture. Sure enough, they stocked some very large, Mexican style, carved wooden spoons that are supposedly used to stir huge kettles of frijoles. Thirteen days later, Nick Carter received an oversized Federal Express pouch with a large wooden spoon and a short note: "Nick, tomorrow will be two weeks. Go down the hall and give the kettle a stir and a sniff. I will call at 10:00 a.m., your time. Let me know how it smells."

Nick took my call, said it smelled good, and that I should get a flight to their offices in Chicago. Weeks later, they locked me in the studio and we produced the audio program. It became the

fastest-selling training album in the telemarketing industry.
I give much of the credit to the synergy created by that spoon
and note.

Medium Efforts

10. Walk meetings.

Instead of sitting down for a meal and taking in extra calories or having another boring office meeting, why not step outside and change the view? Invite somebody you want to visit with to meet you for a beach walk, nature walk, power walk, whatever. Change things up and stay active at the same time. An article in *The Huffington Post* noted, "Walking helps break down formalities, relaxes inhibitions and fosters camaraderie between colleagues—and less eye contact can fuel more personal conversation. Meeting on the go also minimizes distractions—no phones, no email, no texts, no colleagues interrupting you."

11. Network (gracefully).

Use your social calendar as an opportunity to put yourself in new environments and social circles. It's okay to share with others what you do and how you can be of service, but just remember: Be gracious and respectful of your environment. Don't go into a major sales pitch.

12. Send treats as a warm way to start a conversation.

Pick ten people to whom you want to send a tiny treat just to check in and say hello. Sending a small treat often works as a pleasant opening to start a conversation. For example: Share a playlist of your favorite tunes or put it on a flash drive to give to others, an ornament, or a copy of your favorite book. The goal here is to share a warm and friendly gesture that helps you stand out from the masses. Note: Only do what represents your style and your voice.

13. Create a dining experience and pick up the check.

When inviting people to a good old-fashioned breakfast, lunch, or dinner, pick a place with a little flair, a place where people want to go—like that new hot place that everyone's been dying to check out. Invite other interesting people to join you to spice up the conversation and create an experience for the attendees that they will be talking about for weeks to come. Maybe even invite a special guest to join you, like a local celebrity or a thought leader in your industry who will intrigue people and make them want to attend.

14. Customized gifts unique to your brand can reinforce your messaging.

To leave a favorable impression in the minds of television, radio, and print media professionals I met with while promoting my last book, I would send a special customized box of healthy chocolates that were designed to match the elements of the book cover. My publicist received countless e-mails from people afterward who commented on how much they appreciated the gesture and how rarely they received thank-yous from authors after interviews. Hopefully this will leave a favorable impression and encourage them to book me again in the future.

15. Don't just get a booth at a trade show—really stand out.

Find a unique way to encourage individuals to enter your trade show booth space so that you can creatively tell your story and then convert that into the next appointment time.

Medium Example: Ryan Kelly and the Dollar Tulip Trade Show Booth Story

Financial adviser Ryan Kelly was just starting out in investment management and striving to build his client portfolio when his family's small firm decided to attend a trade show.

"I needed to stand out from the big name-brand competitors at this large show, but we didn't have a big, fancy booth or even a beautiful five-dollar brochure to hand out. . . . It was tough to compete." Ryan came up with a scrappy idea in order to capture the attention of passersby inspired by the legendary story of the value of a tulip. Here's the story:

> *In Holland in 1636, one rare tulip costs four bushels of wheat, eight pigs, twelve sheep, five kegs of beer, a thousand pounds of cheese, a bed, a fine suit, and a silver cup. Imagine the following scenario: That same year, the captain of a ship carrying foreign cargo sees an interesting-looking "onion" that he thinks looks out of place among the fine silks they are transporting. The "onion" was a tulip, but the captain, not understanding what it was or its value, ate it with his lunch. When the ship arrives on shore, the captain is thrown in jail for almost a year for eating a tulip that would have paid for the captain's ship and fed the crew for a year.*

If the captain had known the value of the tulip, he surely would not have eaten it. The following year that same tulip had lost 95 percent of its value and would trade for only the cost of one sheep. . . .

Back to the trade show . . .

Ryan taught himself to make dozens of origami tulip flowers from real one-dollar bills and then arranged them in a "tulip bouquet" as a display. As people passed by the trade show booth he would ask them if they had received their "Dollar Bill Tulip" yet. He would then share the story, and a little about himself and the service he provides. He would give them the tulip, which included his contact information and a small note that read: "At Spectrum, we know the difference between an overpriced tulip and a sound investment. . . . Our goal is to earn your business and construct a strategy designed for your specific needs. . . ."

His approach was unique, intriguing, and effective.

Large Efforts

16. Hire a ride or provide the ride.

     Going to the same party or event? Add a touch of class and offer to go together in style. Hiring a chauffeur or car can allow more connection time to and from the event—not to mention it can be safer. Not in the budget? Offer to be the designated driver and provide the selfless service of forgoing the open bar to have the time with those select passengers! Offer to take someone to the airport. It will give you some alone time in the car with them to connect along the way.

17. Integrate your activities.

Life is busy for everyone these days. Why not try to mix a little business with family when appropriate? Going to an outdoor concert in the park? Invite a client and their family to join you and yours. Catching an opening night at the movies? Extend the invitation to a business contact. We have to make an effort to be more social in today's Internet-focused world, so ask. Even if they say, "No, thank you," you will be remembered for the thought.

18. Create an event.

Another great way to put the spotlight on yourself is to sponsor events with others or on your own. The event serves as the vehicle through which you introduce who you are and what your intentions are to expand your base of contacts. Many people won't realize they need you or your service, product, or idea until they attend the event and learn more about you. And don't worry, options abound. You can host a party, sponsor a training event or seminar, or sponsor a hole at a golf tournament. You can even volunteer to work pro bono at an event to gain access to new and wonderful opportunities. Find the unique gatherings and meetings in your specific industry that few people know about. Dig, dig, dig.

19. Treat your guests to a special outing.

Take your clients to a concert, golf outing, tennis match, charity event—something people would love to attend but typically don't splurge for on their own or can't get access to. They may be more excited about attending the event than about spending time with you, but that's okay. It opens the door and buys you more time to connect with them.

20. Create a reason to celebrate.

Use a person's ten-year anniversary with their company, the closing of a big deal, or any other special occasion to engage in celebration. Sending a bottle of champagne (alcoholic or non-alcoholic) just puts a little extra attention on a special time in someone's life and will be noticed and appreciated.

21. Build a customized personal Web site.

In a world where job applications are increasingly being sub-mitted online, how does a candidate stand out as unique? How do you get scrappy in the digital world? Sam Richter suggests applying online but including a link to a customized personal Web site that features a three-minute video of you sharing the reasons you would be a perfect fit for the job. He recommends keeping it simple and easy. There are Web sites that can help you build unique-looking Web pages and the cost is negligible. You don't have to know a lot about technology to create a great-looking site or page.

Large Example: Nina Mufleh and the Airbnb Job Application Story

Consider the story of Nina Mufleh. Her dream was to work at Airbnb, but like countless others navigating the job market, she was getting nowhere fast with traditional online approaches. Nothing she'd tried—e-mails, job listings, phone calls—had worked. So she de-cided to attack the problem from an entirely new angle.

She designed an online résumé that mirrored Airbnb's Web site, right down to the square text boxes, tiny customized icons, and inviting photos. She didn't focus on her past experience but on what she knows about the travel industry and her perspective on how the company could consider expanding its market in the future. It took a week to complete, and she employed the assistance of a designer she'd worked with at a previous job to pull it all together.

Mufleh submitted the résumé with the following note: "I want to work at Airbnb. I realize thousands of other very talented people do as well, so to show the kind of value I'd bring to the team, I've decided to be proactive and have analyzed the global tourism market to give you my two cents on where Airbnb should focus next." Mufleh's résumé began attracting attention—particularly from Airbnb CEO Brian Chesky and CMO Jonathan Mildenhall—almost immediately. Her efforts paid off, and she scored an interview with the company.

BE CURIOUS

Now that you have had a chance to take a look at these twenty-one different ideas used by others on the scrappy path, I hope you're feeling activated and inspired. Imagine the possibilities when you apply a similar strategy to your situation. While you will need to tweak and adjust these ideas to your own unique circumstances, keep your mind open to new possibilities and remember that great ideas don't grow in infertile soil. The nuances of a brilliant effort are most often found hidden within the most obvious concepts. That's why your homework is so integral to the design. You want to have a general idea of all the different scrappy actions worth considering and then take the time to look further at the details. That's when it gets good. This is why your curiosity about the person you want to meet or connect with is so important. If you're not genuinely curious about him or her, how will you uncover anything of true value to apply to your situation? The beauty of a scrappy execution is in the little things—otherwise it's just like everyone else's efforts.

My friend and colleague Roy Freiman, who is the vice president of strategy and analytics at a financial institution, had this to say about the nature of being scrappy: "Scrappy people demonstrate intellectual curiosity through action. They anticipate, think, and amend."

Brian Grazer and Charles Fishman put forth a similar idea in their book *A Curious Mind: The Secret to a Bigger Life.* "One of the joys of curiosity is its power to transform your life." They encourage readers to engage in curious conversations without a specific agenda—just to listen, explore, understand a different perspective, and learn. The same principle applies to getting scrappy.

THE IDEAS WILL COME

If you're feeling stuck and having a difficult time coming up with some fresh and unique ideas to move you toward your goal, don't panic. I strongly recommend going back to the previous chapter and walking through each of the prep work elements again. It's normal to get stuck, but to get unstuck, you have to be willing to brainstorm and cultivate ideas from scratch.

Brainstorming ideas involves building a team and surrounding yourself with talented people willing to go the distance with you. Like networking when doing your homework, brainstorming with a team is a great way to bounce crazy ideas off one another and feed off a mutual energy. Sometimes you don't know what you don't know and you need an outside and fresh perspective other than your own so you can see situations through a different lens. Sometimes you are too close to a project to see a simple answer.

If you're still at a loss about your next move, sleep on it or take a shower. Relax into the process. Time pressure can be good, but intensely stressful situations can block creativity.

If you have ever had a moment of clarity while in the shower, you're not alone. In a 2012 study conducted at the University of California, Santa Barbara, participants who performed undemanding activities that allowed their minds to wander experienced a significant increase in creative problem-solving abilities. The relaxing environment and familiar routine of a shower is a great opportunity to let your mind work on autopilot. Demanding activities, like solving a word or math problem, didn't have the same effect, so put aside thoughts of specific worries, problems, or annoyances as you're getting ready to hop into the shower.

In a curious conversation with my talented and creative friend Bill Stainton (a winner of twenty-nine Emmy awards in the field of entertainment for writing, producing, and performing and a former writer for *The Tonight Show* with Jay Leno) on this theory about your shower being a personal idea booth, he agrees that something magical happens in the shower (stay with me here . . .) that relaxes your brain and ultimately provides the perfect environment for creative ideas to emerge. Here are a few of Bill's pearls of wisdom on why the shower is a great place to generate ideas:

- Showers tend to be relaxing and stress free. Have you ever noticed that when you're stuck in a traffic jam while late for an important appointment it's very difficult to be creative (except perhaps in your use of language)? Yes, we all know people who insist, "I do my best work under pressure," but most of us use it as an excuse for procrastination. The truth is that, in general, extreme stress is the enemy of creativity. So the next time you're in your nice hot shower . . . chill out!

- Showers give you uninterrupted time. Showers tend to provide blissful "alone" time with no distractions, which provides a perfect setting for creativity.

- It's routine and mindless so your thoughts are free to wander. Most of us can make it through pretty much the entire shower process without having to think about it. That means it's recess for our brain! Our minds are free to wander from thought to thought, which is how creative connections occur. At the same time, our minds are free to wonder: "What would happen if . . . ?," "How would my smartest competitor solve this problem?," "Do I really have to repeat after lathering and rinsing?"

- It's a safe place. It's really hard to be creative when you're being chased by a bear. Fortunately, that rarely happens in today's modern showers. The shower is a safe place, and in a safe place we can let our guard down. When we're no longer worried about becoming a serving of Purina Bear Chow, we can let the creativity flow.

- You tend to shower when you're tired. When do you take your shower? Typically, it's either first thing in the morning or last thing at night. Either way . . . you're a little bit tired—and research shows that that's the ideal time to come up with creative ideas. Haven't you ever had an "aha!" moment just as you're drifting off to sleep, or the moment you wake up? That's because when the brain is just a little fuzzy, the self-censorship mode (that mode that keeps telling you, "That's a stupid idea!") takes a break. The compartment walls fall away, and your mind can start to see connections that were closed off when you were wide awake.

- Your shower is a natural white noise generator. Research has found that a low volume of meaningless background noise actually enhances our creative abilities. When it comes to "low-volume, meaningless background noise," nothing beats white noise! Because "white noise" and "shower noise" are virtually indistinguishable, you've got a perfect little creativity booth!

- It's not your workplace! When you're in the workplace, your brain tends to go into "work" mode . . . but creativity thrives best in "play" mode. So that's why, quite often, the best thing you can do to generate creative ideas is to get away from the workplace environment.

So think of your shower as your personal idea booth. Oh, and to answer that question that's been on your mind ever since reason #3: No, you do not have to repeat after lathering and rinsing. You're welcome.

DO THE BEST YOU CAN WITH WHAT YOU'VE GOT

As you can see from the stories and examples in this chapter, a person with a scrappy mindset isn't one who sits back and waits for the pieces to fall into place or for a lucky break to present itself. A scrapper takes deliberate and thoughtful action to create opportunities where few or even none existed before. Sometimes you have to do the best you can with the knowledge you have at that given moment. Sometimes it doesn't require a massive amount of homework— sometimes it does.

But what if you don't have time to do weeks of preparation or craft a long-term approach for your scrappy strategy? I certainly understand that some of you may have picked up this book because you have an immediate problem to solve. In that case, do the best you can with the time and resources you have available. Act quickly if necessary, but think long-term. That way, you will be prepared when another opportunity arises.

As we have discussed throughout the book, a savvy effort, whether small, medium, or large, draws positive attention. Most people enjoy a pleasant surprise, and I believe successful people tend to gravitate toward smart, scrappy, and classy gestures. They get it. Decision makers in positions of power are usually a bit more forgiving, even when the effort is a little bumpy. They respect people who get a little scrappy and make allowances for them. Odds are they have been in a similar position.

This entire section on developing a strategy was created to help you think through the many different options you can consider as you craft your plan *before* you actually execute. You have learned how to dig in and do your homework, evaluate your timing, hone your skills, and cultivate new ideas. It might take two or three approaches to figure out the best one. If you are apprehensive, that's okay. You have to try. At this point, you should be able to clearly define your goal and customize the approach you will take to reach it. You are ready to stand out and dazzle those in your path.

REVIEW

- In order for you to earn the attention of a listener, and create an opportunity for yourself in the process, the recipient must be pleasantly surprised.

- It's important to customize your effort in a way that makes the receiver happy. It's not about what you want. It doesn't have to make sense to everyone, just you and the recipient of your effort.

- Evaluate whether your effort is going to be small, medium, or large in scale. Sometimes your idea or solution to a problem is a simple, easy-to-execute effort. Small actions can have a big impact too. But again, sometimes the big ideas get the big results.

- The nuances of a brilliant effort are often hidden within the most obvious concepts and in the details. That's when it gets good—otherwise your actions are just like everyone else's. That's why your curiosity about the person you want to meet or connect with is so important.

- If you get stuck, that's okay. You can go back and review the prep work discussed in the previous chapter, brainstorm with a team, or go take a shower.

- Do the best you can with the time and resources you have available. Act quickly if necessary, but think long-term. That way, you will be prepared when another opportunity arises.

Chapter Activity: Brainstorm three ideas—one small, one medium, and one large. Think through the process we have walked through in the last three chapters. You have set your goal, identified the appropriate receiver, established the best time to execute your plan, and done the prep work. Now it's time to refine your ideas and concepts to focus on a specific strategy.

Small Scrappy Idea:

- -
- -
- -

Medium Scrappy Idea:

- -
- -
- -

Large Scrappy Idea:

- -
- -
- -

What's Next: Before you actually execute your strategy and take action, it's wise to consider the crash-and-burn stories of those who have gone before you—or what I call "good ideas gone bad."

Part 3

EXECUTION

Scrappy *execution* is about putting your plan of action into play. It's the "go" phase—the transition from planning into actual engagement, moving forward on a course of action you have developed. This is where the risk comes in, but so does the reward.

This section is divided into four chapters in support of the execution of your strategy. Chapter 7 helps you assess your risk tolerance and avoid the failures of those who have gone before you. Chapter 8 discusses scaling a scrappy culture and strategy within a company or organization. Chapters 9 and 10 put it all together and will encourage you to leave room for serendipity, review a Scrappy Strategy Action Plan Checklist, and leave you with a few inspiring scrappy stories.

Chapter 7

RISK, MISTAKES, AND AVOIDING FAILURE

When you take risks you learn that there will be times when you succeed and there will be times when you fail, and both are equally important.

—**Ellen DeGeneres**

WHETHER YOUR GOAL IS TO INFLUENCE A DECISION MAKER or to push yourself beyond where you have gone before, being scrappy is inherently risky. Everyone wants to come up with that spot-on gesture that's just the right amount of funny, daring, confident, and inspiring. But sometimes a person's excitement can override logic. Or, put another way, good ideas can go bad, and quickly. The reality is most ideas that crash and burn originate from a positive and genuine place, but somehow along the way, things go awry. To avoid that, you will want to assess your risk tolerance. How risky is too risky? In this section, we will explore stories of efforts that failed—some quite miserably! It is a cautionary section that will ask you to think through your ideas before you execute. You will learn about some of the most common mistakes people make when getting scrappy, how to assess your personal risk tolerance, and how to anticipate failures before you launch. Finally, you will discover that there can indeed be life after failure.

IDEAS: KEEP, MORPH, OR DELETE

When you open up your mind to the notion of executing a scrappy strategy, the ideas start flowing, and it can be difficult to know what to keep and what to discard. Don't be alarmed or embarrassed if you start entertaining a few crazy ideas. It happens. Your brain is up against the wall and working overtime, generating new and wonderful ways to make things happen. Sometimes a little crazy enters the mix. The key is recognizing when an idea is a bad choice and determining whether or not you can morph it into something else, or scrap it altogether.

For example, let's say your challenge has been to get an appointment to meet with the CEO of this up-and-coming athletic clothing firm to pitch your company as their new marketing consultant. You have been brainstorming and you are totally in the zone, when you think to yourself, "What if I ship myself there inside a crate and pop out and introduce myself? That will get me past the gatekeeper, right?"

This idea, by the way, is completely insane. But, believe it not, it has been attempted. You might have even heard about the guy who shipped himself in a FedEx container to a girlfriend as a romantic surprise. Tragically, it is not an urban legend, and he almost suffocated to death in the process. There are countless stories out there of people stuffing themselves into crates and boxes and attempting to get mailed across the country. Please do not do this. Not only is it dangerous, it is illegal, in any form, to mail a person.

It's okay to be spontaneous, even a little silly, but think it through. Put yourself in the mind of the recipient. What would you think if somebody did what you're considering? Personally, I would freak out if somebody arrived in a box to surprise me—it's creepy.

So what are some good rules to follow when you find yourself bombarded with ideas? Apply common sense. Avoid the crazy, dumb stunts that can harm you or get you into trouble—criminal or otherwise. Excitement and surprise certainly have their place, but nothing tops sophisticated and tasteful. Finally, make sure your effort is one that you can be proud of in the future. The best scrappy stories are the ones you are happy to share.

WHAT IS YOUR RISK TOLERANCE?

> *If you are not willing to risk the unusual, you will have to settle for the ordinary.*
>
> **—Jim Rohn**

To minimize the risk of failure, you will want to determine your risk tolerance. The risk factor upon executing your scrappy strategy should be evaluated after you have brainstormed several ideas. For example, on a scale from one to ten, one being no risk, ten being high risk, how bold are you willing to be with your effort? Some people are willing to take on greater risk than others. (I personally choose low-risk options, but there are others who push the envelope and walk directly into the "disruptive zone.") You may want to ask yourself how much adversity you are willing to face before moving forward.

Not long ago I had a great coffee chat about this specific element of getting scrappy with Jared Cohen, president of Jigsaw, former director of Google Ideas, and an adjunct senior fellow at the Council on Foreign Relations. For someone who hasn't even reached his mid-thirties, Jared has led quite the scrappy life. He's a Rhodes Scholar, a former adviser to secretaries of state Condoleezza Rice and Hillary Clinton, and one of *Time*'s 100 Most Influential People in 2013. He knows a thing or two about forging headlong into adversity when most people would back off.

Here are four key perspectives that Jared shared and we discussed during our conversation:

1. When you consider getting scrappy, know that this effort is going to present you with what could be called the Scrappy Artist's Dilemma, the notion that you are basically making a commitment to not play by the rules. That commitment comes with a bit of risk. (This notion is a different take on the Artist's Dilemma, which suggests that the life of an artist is a constant struggle between creative control and financial reward.)

2. If you get scrappy, you have to accept the fact that not everybody is going to like you. In fact, along the way, you could run into four types of adversaries:

   First, you will meet those people who are threatened by you or your actions. How do you turn them around? You present them with a value proposition.

Second, there are those who are substantively skeptical and accuse you of being "all flash, no pan." (Referring to the old saying "a flash in the pan"—they simply doubt that you have any solid basis.) The only way to win this group over is to put points on the board. Show them a win.

Third, some might want to take you down simply because they want to win and want you to lose. Again, putting points on the board—specifically, more than they are—is the only way to beat them.

Fourth, sometimes those who are more senior than you—in age, experience and position—will oppose your efforts. Chances are they are never going to accept you no matter what you try. They don't want you coming in and attempting to take over their territory. The only way to beat them is to isolate them and their ideas and turn them into lone wolves. This is a long-term play—a long-term antidote to wait them out. Sometimes it takes two years, sometimes it takes five years, but you just wait them out. Eventually they will leave and you will stay.

3. When executing a scrappy strategy, one of three things can happen: either you piss people off, nothing will happen at all, or you're going to get a win. If you piss people off, then you've gone too far and you need to pull back. If nothing happens at all, you have to try harder. And if you win, you win. You're moving the intention forward and it's all good.

4. If you're trying to get scrappy in an organization, the best thing you can do is to bring ideas—don't bring drama.

These pearls of wisdom from Jared can be very helpful when you're determining your comfort level and figuring out how far you're willing to push your intention forward after weighing all the possible challenges you may face along the way.

STAY TRUE TO YOUR BRAND AND PERSONALITY

Whatever your effort, make sure it's a true reflection of who you are. It has to match your personality, your brand—and your audience— if it's going to land. When you attempt something that's completely out of character or just the wrong fit, people will notice and your message and intent can be quickly overshadowed by awkwardness and discomfort. It's okay to be daring and push the envelope, but never lose sight of your end goal. If you're going for the "wow factor," strive to be a positive disrupter instead of merely disruptive. Getting attention simply for the sake of getting attention is not going to help you. Remember that what works for someone else might not work for you. Take the big, bold brands of Madonna, Eminem, or Lady Gaga. Now think about Taylor Swift, Carrie Underwood, or Josh Groban. Taylor Swift would not do what Lady Gaga would do—and neither should you. Or take the adventure-seeking brand of Red Bull energy drinks. It would never take the same approach as, say, the homespun brand of Snapple beverages. The pitch would not resonate with its core customer base.

The good news is that Red Bull doesn't have to emulate Snapple because there's room for both brands to do it their own way. Scrappiness exists as a spectrum or range of options rather than as a bucket of predetermined efforts that everyone chooses from. This range is accommodating to all kinds of personalities, styles, comfort levels, and humor. It's up to you to decide where you fit on the continuum and how far you're willing to drift in either direction.

Imagine the idea of getting scrappy existing as a range with a pendulum. It can swing not only from side to side, but in a full circle or somewhere in the middle (depending on your risk tolerance and how much information you have before you take action on your effort). It's important to remember that this pendulum also might swing to a stop on multiple sections of the circle. For instance, it's entirely possible for you to be bold and classy. In general, where do you think you would show up?

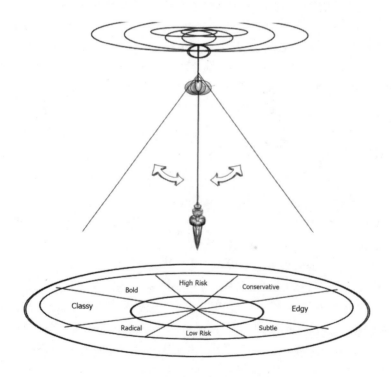

Take my friend Randy Gage. He's definitely scrappy, but his *kind* of scrappy is the polar opposite of mine. As an author and strategic marketing adviser, his style epitomizes brash and bold, and he's all about pushing the boundaries. With Randy, you know what you're getting right up front. He's outspoken and unconventional, and his brand follows suit. And that's okay—the scrappy spectrum has plenty of room for both of us.

To further illustrate this point, let me share with you a conversation I had with Randy about one particularly over-the-top promotion he staged to boost attendance at a three-day marketing boot camp he was teaching with a colleague.

There were dozens of other companies and promoters offering workshops and seminars, so Randy wanted to break through the clutter. To do so, he created a direct mail campaign that centered on a really bulky envelope containing . . . an adult diaper. He included a letter explaining that his boot camp was going to help recipients get fabulous response rates from their direct marketing, Internet marketing, and other efforts. "Hey, once you see the response rates we're getting from our ideas, you're gonna crap your pants."

Yes, he did that. And not only did he send them that diaper to get their attention, but the letter said that when they arrived at the actual event he would give them an entire box of the diapers to wear for the three days of the boot camp. (And he really had a stack at the registration table!) It was just an idea to take a little risk, to be a little edgy, cut through the white noise and say, "This is not a normal, boring marketing seminar taught by some college marketing professor who's never actually marketed anything. This is a bold, edgy event, conducted by guys who are actually in the space, doing it successfully, and you need to be there." And as a result, he sold out that event.

While I would have worried that someone might be offended, Randy didn't. In his mind, there's always the potential to offend someone, and you can't cater to that all the time. As he said, "My advice is if you are really out to do something extraordinary, don't worry about getting some 'haters.' Worry if you don't. If you don't have anybody criticizing you, ridiculing you, or anyone who is a hater, I don't think you've attempted anything extraordinary."

Randy's crazy scrappy idea worked for him, but when I asked him if he could picture me doing it, he couldn't stop laughing. The reason Randy cracked up was because he understood how absurd it would be for me to pull a stunt like that. He knows me and my brand, is familiar with my more conservative image, and appreciates how inappropriate that would be for me and my style. Truth be told, I think that if I sent that out to my clients, I would likely upset a lot of people—people who couldn't wait to tell me they didn't want to do business with me anymore. Again, that doesn't make the adult diaper mail-out right or wrong, it just means that it's not the right fit for me.

This disruptive idea worked for Randy, but as we move forward, you need to truly contemplate whether such a strategy would work for you, your style, your brand, and the recipient of your gesture. How would they interpret your effort? Asking these questions and determining your risk tolerance is part of doing your due diligence.

I asked Randy in closing if he thought getting scrappy was a risky play.

He said, "No, I think *not* getting scrappy is a risky play."

COMMON SCRAPPY MISTAKES TO AVOID

Here are a few examples of common mistakes people have made when attempting to get scrappy:

- Telling a lie to make something happen
- Sending an inappropriate gift
- Dropping by unannounced or uninvited
- Breaking the law to obtain access
- Making a poor judgment call
- Playing dirty
- Missing the window of opportunity
- Overreaching and setting unrealistic expectations
- Scaring the prospect
- Pushing too hard or not knowing when to back off
- Failing to consider the outcome or possible negative consequences

It's quite possible you have made or will make a few of these mistakes at some point—that's why they're common. These errors tend to happen when we take shortcuts instead of putting in the real work. Life is busy, messy, and distracting, and you are bound to have missteps along the way. The key is being aware of some of these mistakes before you make them, and a good way to do that is to examine other people's bloopers—from a safe distance, of course.

Take a closer look at how some of these misguided attempts can unfold and the negative effect they can have on your overall success.

Making a Poor Judgment Call

For all of Steven Schussler's success with Schussler Creative and developing hit restaurants like Rainforest Café, T-REX, The Boathouse at Disney World, Galaxy Drive In, and more, he has crashed and burned quite a few times.

Consider this cringe-worthy example: (Thanks again, Steven, for graciously allowing me to share your misstep with the world.)

When Steven was twenty-one years old, he was trying hard to make a name for himself selling advertising for a small talk radio station in Miami, Florida. He set his sights on the Coca-Cola Company, specifically the chairman of the board, and would not be deterred. One day, after maybe fifteen calls, he managed to get the chairman's secretary to divulge that he would be in an all-day meeting in an auditorium. Then Steven let his imagination off the leash in a move as audacious as it was original.

> I decided that I was going to walk into the middle of five thousand people in an auditorium and tell everybody that it was the chairman of the board's birthday . . . even though it wasn't. And I was going to get five thousand people to help me sing him "Happy Birthday" while I walked a birthday cake to the stage.

Steven figured he would at least get to shake the man's hand, and even if he was upset, it would be a way to get in the door. "I did it. I did it and he was pissed, okay? He was really upset by it. And it took a couple of months for him to get over the fact that I sang him

'Happy Birthday' in front of five thousand people and interrupted his event."

Needless to say, the chairman of the board didn't see the humor in Steven's gesture. So Steven began working to set things right. He apologized weekly with letters and phone calls. "At first he got mad and later mad turned to endearing. And eventually I got to a lunch that he was at and we sat down, and we talked and he accepted my apologies . . . he eventually called his advertising agency and said, 'Give the kid an order. Give the kid an order.'"

Sure, Steven ultimately turned this into a win, but only because a great deal of time had passed. He was genuinely remorseful and the guy obviously had a soft spot for a kid scrambling to make it in the business.

Pushing Too Hard or Not Knowing When to Back Off

On one hand, it's good to get scrappy and creative, but there can be a point of no return. Sometimes "no" really means no. If the decision maker you are approaching says "thanks, but no thanks" repeatedly, you have to respect their wishes. When you persist past the point of several firm rejections, it creeps into inappropriate behavior. Toni Ko, who founded NYX Cosmetics at the age of twenty-six with little business experience, a tight budget, and big dreams, is a scrappy woman who appreciates it when people go the extra mile.

However, Toni experienced a scenario where another woman pushed too hard and didn't know when to stop. The young woman began pitching her services for Toni's company in a very determined way. Toni declined because her service wasn't a good fit for NYX Cosmetics, but then began getting little gifts from the woman: a bouquet of roses, a box of chocolates, cookies.... After somehow finding out that Toni had a dog, she even sent pet treats. Toni was flattered and appreciative at first, but sent an e-mail reminding the young woman that her business proposition simply wasn't a good fit for her company. Still she persisted. It took a few attempts to really get the point across to this young woman that Toni wasn't interested. She became bothersome and didn't know when to back off. Her original efforts had lost their charm, and ultimately Toni was more annoyed than impressed.

NO STALKING!

We spent a lot of time in the last section talking about developing ideas and doing your homework, but remember: You are only going to dig as deep as it's appropriate within the context of the professional relationship. If you go farther than that, it's called stalking, and that's creepy. Do not focus on only one person, place, or opportunity. It's never a good idea to put all your eggs in one basket. There are many paths to getting to your desired outcome. Maintain a respectful approach and do not invade the personal privacy of your existing or potential contacts.

Failing to Consider the Outcome or Possible Negative Consequences

Sometimes a good idea can go bad when the timing is off or you haven't fully weighed the repercussions of your effort. British food company Nutricia Ltd. found this out the hard way back in November 2001. It started out with a good, scrappy idea; the plan was to mail out six thousand samples of the company's Glutafin Flour Mix to customers who had requested the product. Who doesn't love getting a free treat in the mail? It's a fun marketing tool, and I think Nutricia was on the right track. The problem was timing. The entire world was on edge following the anthrax letter attacks in the United States. A U.K. postal workers' union quickly blasted the mass mailing as "inappropriate." Although Nutricia Ltd. argued that the flour packets were well sealed and sent only to homes that had requested the product, the workers handling the mail felt differently. Unfortunately, the company didn't think through the repercussions of sending white powder through the mail, and it became a huge public-relations problem and a failed marketing effort.

On a smaller scale, an individual could make a similar mistake. Consider the example of a marketing executive who sent chocolates to a prospect who was allergic. Or the office supply representative who sent a Christmas ornament to a Jewish family who celebrates Hanukkah.

CONDUCT A PREMORTEM TO ANTICIPATE POSSIBLE FAILURES

Once you have evaluated your general risk tolerance and made sure you are avoiding common mistakes, you will find it helpful to examine each idea individually. Assess the risk associated with each effort—how far you are willing to put yourself out there—to help you determine which plan to select before you execute. It's time to conduct a premortem.

Put another way, before moving forward, assume the worst has already happened. Are you willing to deal with the consequences, if any, should your plan crash and burn? Consider the work of scientist and author Gary Klein. He introduced this concept of a "premortem" in 2007, in an article in the *Harvard Business Review*.

> *A premortem is the hypothetical opposite of a postmortem. A postmortem in a medical setting allows health professionals and the family to learn what caused a patient's death. Everyone benefits except, of course, the patient. A premortem in a business setting comes at the beginning of a project rather than the end, so that the project can be improved rather than autopsied. Unlike a typical critiquing session, in which project team members are asked what might go wrong, the premortem operates on the assumption that the "patient" has died, and so asks what did go wrong. The team members' task is to generate plausible reasons for the project's failure.*

Even if you have determined your risk tolerance level, it's still important to be painfully aware of the possibility of failure. Why, you ask? Because it happens all the time. According to the IBM Global Making Change Work Study of 2008, the reality is that an average of 60 percent of projects fail. Those odds can be scary, but there is an upside, and to find it we must consider the reasons behind the failure. One reason is the reluctance of team members—and even leaders—to share objections to a plan. So what might happen if we eliminated that reluctance? What if more people felt empowered to express worries, opposition, and insecurities?

At this point, you might be thinking a premortem is appropriate only for a team, but that's not true. You can use the premortem method to practice responsible scrappiness and think through your actions before embarking on your adventure. By operating on the assumption that your scrappy effort failed, you can examine the reasons behind it one by one. First, let yourself imagine the failure. Second, write down why it failed. After all, you know your plan better than anyone, and chances are you're going to know exactly where you went wrong. Third, take those reasons and study them, identifying the timing of each misstep and how it affects the overall strategy.

This process gives you the power to look into the future and change it. Conducting a premortem enables you to identify negative consequences, problems with execution, and the blunders that keep your scrappy strategy from being lawful, appropriate, safe, or mannerly. It allows you to learn from your mistakes in the least catastrophic way possible. "In the end," Klein says, "a premortem may be the best way to circumvent any need for a painful postmortem."

The story of Doug Hughes is an excellent example of when a premortem could have prevented negative consequences. Hughes, who was a Florida mail carrier, wanted to capture the attention of Congress. He was passionate about "campaign reform legislation" and wanted to deliver 535 letters outlining his call for "an end to the influence of money in politics." In an attempt to be clever and deliver the letters to the members of Congress with flair, Hughes landed a gyrocopter on U.S. Capitol grounds on April 15, 2015. While his effort was indeed interesting and creative, it was also against the law! Although he allegedly notified newspapers and tried to inform government officials of his plan, his strategy was dangerous and he was lucky he wasn't shot out of the sky.

Would you consider this plan a success or a failure? To some, it might appear as if Doug Hughes's effort was a success. After all, his name and story made national news. But is it merely his actions and their threat to national security that are being discussed, or his message? Hughes was not only unable to actually deliver the 535 letters to the members of Congress that day (the police seized his gyrocopter and the bin carrying his protest letters), but he now faces six felony and misdemeanor charges relating to violating restricted airspace.

Since his arrest, Hughes has pleaded not guilty and turned down a ten-month plea deal on lesser charges. If convicted, he could spend almost ten years in prison. Certainly this was not the outcome Doug Hughes was hoping for. He might have assessed his high risk tolerance, but he did not do his homework or conduct a premortem. If he had, I would guess he would have devised an alternative scrappy strategy that ensured his message was heard without breaking multiple federal laws.

LIFE AFTER FAILURE: CAN YOU RECOVER WITH ANOTHER ATTEMPT?

Is there life after failure? Can you recover with another attempt? If you set out on a journey, you will have wins and losses along the way.

Failure is a fact of life, but it doesn't have to signal the end of your quest. Failure—that maddening inability to succeed—often is just the beginning. Crashing and burning is always a possibility, but it's in the recovery that we grow and improve. It's okay to be unfinished, because maybe your idea or message is still cooking, still becoming.

One thing I know for sure about crashing and burning is that sometimes what doesn't work leads you to what does. Consider the story of an amazing young entrepreneur, Carter Kostler, the creator of Define Bottle, which allows consumers to infuse their water with fruit. I first learned about Carter's invention when I was home one Friday night watching television. He was featured on an episode of *Beyond the Tank*, which profiles the stories of people who received deals on the original *Shark Tank* show and those who did not.

The Emmy Award–winning *Shark Tank* is produced by Mark Burnett, who's behind *Survivor* and *The Voice*, and it's based on the Japanese *Dragon's Den* format created by Nippon Television Network Corporation. The show features potential investors, called "sharks," who field pitches from aspiring entrepreneurs seeking financial support for their products and services. The sharks, "all tough, self-made, multi-millionaire and billionaire tycoons," as they are described on the American show's Web site, have one main goal—"to get a return on their investment and own a piece of the next big business idea. When the sharks hear an idea worth sinking their teeth into, they're more than ready to declare war and fight each other for a piece of it." Each episode is filled with the drama, tension, despair, and elation an entrepreneur experiences when reaching for a dream.

Carter appeared on season five of *Shark Tank* at the age of fifteen (which is a pretty impressive scrappy maneuver for a young man of his age in and of itself). During his presentation to the sharks, he explained that he designed Define Bottle when he was only thirteen years old as a way to help his younger brother, Chris, ditch sodas and drink more water:

"I may be young but that does not hold me back from knowing I can make a difference in this world," he said. "So, sharks, who wants to help the world define what they drink?" By the end of Carter's presentation, the sharks seemed genuinely impressed with him. Then the questions began.

"How much have you spent developing it?" Kevin O'Leary asked.

"Three hundred thousand dollars," Carter answered. "My parents have taken out a mortgage on the house." Reaction from the sharks to this debt amount was not good. Carter later explained, "The sharks took the mortgage as a huge red flag . . . and what made it worse was that I was not expecting that!"

One by one, the sharks declined to invest in Define Bottle. "I'm out . . . I'm out . . . I'm out . . . I'm out."

The rejection was devastating. "It really crushed me . . . at that moment," Carter remembered. "I was like, 'Wow, all of them are out. There's no hope for a deal. There's no hope for getting those connections with a shark.'"

And while the sharks did compliment Carter on his presentation and his accomplishments, explaining, "We treated you just like we did anybody of any age. You should be very proud of that," he was understandably disappointed.

Carter was in shock as he walked backstage to meet his parents,

Carla and Mark Weisman. "It was a terrible feeling," he said. "All that tremendous pressure and then—that crash."

Carter's mom said, "When Carter walked out of the tank without a deal, he had a look of total devastation on his face. . . . And it didn't just last a few hours or a day—it stuck with him . . . with all of us . . . for a while, we were down."

His dad added, "I've never seen him that dejected."

For Carter, a scrappy young man from a very young age, the failure to get a deal was a deeply emotional setback. "There were definitely residual effects—for several weeks—of being depressed or thinking about it too much," he said. It took some time, but eventually his scrappy mindset kicked back in. "There was a moment where I said, 'I have to stop [feeling sad about this],'" Carter recalled. "That's when I really kicked it into high gear and said, 'I'm going to get into big box retail on my own'—and I did!"

The Define Bottle's sales began to take off. The company projected earnings of $2 million in one year and $2.5 million the next. Carter got Define Bottle into Target, Dick's Sporting Goods, and on the Home Shopping Network (HSN). Country music star Carrie Underwood even created a design for his product. "I paid off my parents' mortgage, and the weight was off my shoulders," Carter said of his rebound. "Not getting a deal with a shark sucked, but I think this is about triumph and getting over [defeat]. . . . You could say that that failure [on *Shark Tank*] brought me to this point."

Well done, Carter. This is a beautiful illustration of recovering after a scrappy setback and making another attempt that led to success.

Failure should be our teacher, not our undertaker. Failure is delay, not defeat. It is a temporary detour, not a dead end. Failure is something we can avoid only by saying nothing, doing nothing, and being nothing.

—Denis Waitley

PLAY SMART AS YOU MOVE FORWARD

As I mentioned in the opening, this is a cautionary chapter designed to help you think through your ideas while developing your strategy before you execute. You will save a great deal of time, money, and sanity if you pause for a bit and consider the stories of efforts that failed. I'm not trying to scare you or discourage you from taking action, but I want you to play smart and consider all of the things that can go wrong as well as the things that can go right and morph your plan when necessary. Review the common mistakes people make when getting scrappy, assess your personal risk tolerance, and anticipate failures before you launch. And remember, even if things don't go the way you had hoped for or planned, there can indeed be life after failure. Then line up your options and give each one a hard look. How do you choose which plan to go with? Good question. Most scrappy individuals say it typically leads back to a simple gut check. The strategy you choose is the one that you believe in your heart and mind will change the game and make the difference. Trust your instincts. Get scrappy, but don't be irresponsible. Make the move you know you would regret *not making*—even if you fail.

REVIEW

- Review all of your scrappy brainstorming ideas and break them down. What do you want to keep, morph, or delete?
- When you begin generating ideas on how to execute a scrappy strategy, sometimes a little crazy enters the mix. Just remember to keep it classy and scrappy and recognize when your creative ideas slide into the realm of bad choices.
- To minimize the risk of failure, you will want to sincerely assess your risk tolerance. On a scale from one to ten, one being no risk, ten being high risk, how bold are you willing to be with your effort?
- Whatever your effort, make sure it's a true reflection of who you are. It has to match your personality, your brand—and your audience—if it's going to land.
- Review and avoid the Most Common Scrappy Mistakes before developing your plan.
- Before executing your plan, conduct a premortem of your strategy to avoid negative outcomes.
- You can recover after a crash and burn. It's okay to be unfinished, because maybe your idea or message is still cooking, still becoming. Sometimes what doesn't work leads you to what does.

Chapter Activity: In the last chapter activity, you were asked to brainstorm three ideas—one small, one medium, and one large. Before you execute on your strategy, consider the following:

1. Review the common mistakes people make when getting scrappy.
2. Assess your personal risk tolerance. Where are you on the spectrum?
3. Do a premortem. Line up your options and give each one a hard look. Let yourself imagine each idea failing. What could go wrong?

   a. Write down why each idea might have failed. After all, you know your plans better than anyone, and chances are you're able to determine where they might go wrong.

   b. Evaluate the challenges and possible negative outcomes and study them. Identify the timing of each misstep and how it affects the overall strategy.

4. Rework your concepts, and when you're comfortable with the risk tolerance level of possible outcomes, you're ready to go!

This process gives you the power to look into the future and change it. How do you choose which plan to go with? Trust your instincts.

What's Next: Sometimes it's necessary to encourage the idea of getting scrappy across a large group of people to adapt to or change circumstances. Up next: how to scale a scrappy culture and strategy within an organization.

Getting in the Ring—Bonus Scrappy Success Story #4

WHEN PLAYING SMALL IS THE RISKY MOVE

SOMETIMES IN A MORE CONSERVATIVE ENVIRONMENT, YOU wind up thinking the conservative approach is the one to take. That's not always the case. Consider the field of education research—heavily documented, fueled by long-standing reputations, and often skeptical of innovators. Right? Sure, but that doesn't always mean playing it safe will move you forward.

Zeynep Young, founder and past CEO of Double Line Partners, an Austin, Texas–based technology services company that serves the K–12 education sector, found this out the hard way. About two years after she started the company, it was still a small outfit—only five people—but they had successfully created a unique method of capturing data about students that could empower teachers to better personalize education. "We were all super passionate about this idea and the fact that it was really disruptive and innovative, and we thought that it could drive a lot of benefits for students."

Soon Double Line got an opportunity to participate in a project in a state that was doing important work in their particular field of education research. Zeynep and her team wanted to go for it, but they were worried their company was too specialized and wouldn't be taken seriously. Finally, they stopped dithering and decided to submit a proposal to land the account. When they received the application, all of the original insecurities returned because the process was extensive and demanding.

"We were concerned that we couldn't meet the application requirements, that we needed a bigger name and history attached to our proposal in order to get the deal. We were concerned that we were too small and couldn't survive the application process on our own."

So Double Line attached itself to a larger, more traditional company, agreeing to hand over 5 percent off the top if it won the project. Zeynep and her team were even kind of proud of themselves, thinking they were being not only realistic but clever in their approach. "We basically agreed to have a partner on paper because they were not actually going to do any of the work. They were just going to be the name on the contract, so we could use their reputation and financial history to boost our credibility."

The plan worked, and Double Line won the project. Zeynep and her team were thrilled, convinced their "innovative" approach was the right one.

But what was really surprising is that once we started delivering the project, the client shared that our agreement with the larger, more established firm actually was a red flag and worked against us during the application process. He explained that it cost us some points and caused them to question whether we were going to be as innovative as they had expected.

It was a powerful lesson to hear that. It made us realize how dangerous it can be to doubt yourself when you're on the verge of trusting your skills and making a big play. Because of our doubt, we chose to play it safe and small. But that decision proved to be the actual risk, and it almost cost us the opportunity.

That moment of awakening was a turning point for Zeynep and Double Line, and it set a critical precedent. From that point on, they knew they could really handle the big project proposals and opportunities on their own. "Now we always play bigger. Win or lose, it just makes more sense."

Chapter 8

SCALING A SCRAPPY CULTURE AND STRATEGY WITHIN AN ORGANIZATION

Hey T, I've been several places speaking over the last couple of weeks and keep hearing "scrappy." In fact, the chief retail officer with Caribou Coffee was just using it to describe how they stay competitive against Starbucks.

—Simon T. Bailey

THE EMPHASIS OF THIS BOOK UP UNTIL THIS POINT HAS BEEN to discuss how an individual's scrappy attitude, effort, strategy, and execution can change his or her circumstances. That said, sometimes it's necessary to encourage the idea of getting scrappy across a large group of people within an organization to adapt to or change circumstances as well.

As a leadership platform, inspiring a scrappy culture can be a great strategy to help increase production and generate business. So how do you add a little scrappy attitude to your organization's culture? It doesn't happen overnight and it can't be mandated, but it can be cultivated over time.

In this chapter we will explore what makes an organization scrappy, examine a specific example of how one organization built a scrappy culture, and provide suggestions on how to adopt a scrappy philosophy within your team, company, or association.

WHAT MAKES AN ORGANIZATION SCRAPPY?

If you stop to think about it, I believe you will find that larger-scale scrappy efforts—put forth by a group, business, or any other type of organization—are a response to dealing with challenging circumstances or events, in the same way as they are for an individual.

The question is: Is there a common denominator within companies or organizations that have fostered a scrappy culture? The answer is yes. It seems the common denominator is somehow typically tied to the leadership within the organization. It does not grow from the field up—it is inspired from the top and infused into the culture.

The CEO, senior management, or leaders:

1. Are willing to get their hands dirty and literally get in the game with the team. They employ scrappy efforts themselves.
2. Foster an environment of creative freedom to execute ideas.
3. Recruit, cultivate, and support talent that thrives in a scrappy environment.
4. Nurture and develop what others might consider "rogue" talent.

Do scrappy individuals make good leaders? It's possible. Just because somebody is scrappy doesn't necessarily mean that person is going to be a great leader—but a strong leader with scrappy qualities is a great combination if you want to build a scrappy environment.

Consider the following case study of a company that developed a scrappy culture from scratch. Tom Bardenett, former president of Crossroads Hospitality, a select-service division of Interstate Hotels & Resorts, successfully built a scrappy culture within his organization. As you will see, this example evolves and is maintained for more than a decade.

Case Study: How Crossroads Hospitality/Interstate Hotels & Resorts Built a Scrappy Culture

Company Profile: Crossroads Hospitality, a division of Interstate Hotels & Resorts

Interstate Hotels & Resorts is a leading global hotel management company with more than 460 hotels and more than 81,000 rooms located throughout the United States and around the world. Interstate is a wholly owned subsidiary of a joint venture between Thayer Lodging Group and Jin Jiang Hotels. Interstate is the largest third-party manager of hotels and resorts in the country and has been for more than fifty years. Crossroads Hospitality is a division of Interstate Hotels & Resorts, specializing in what is called the "select-service market," which represents independent owners, brand affiliation such as Courtyard by Marriott, Residence Inn, Hilton, Starwood, and more. (Select-service hotels are hotels with limited food and beverages versus full-service hotels that have room service, large meeting spaces, convention halls, and a variety of different things to do at the hotel.) More than 50 percent of the Interstate Hotels & Resorts hotels are under the Crossroads Hospitality umbrella.

What They Sell: Crossroads serves as a hotel managing partner for REITs, private equity firms, and high net worth investors. Under a franchise model in the hotel industry, Crossroads Hospitality works as the actual manager of the hotels, and the associates of the hotels are technically employed by Crossroads. The owner pays a fee to Crossroads to run the hotel property entirely.

(In simple terms, let's say you own a small boutique, independent hotel and it's lovely. But it's really becoming a challenge to manage all of the people, the staffing, the taxes, and other miscellaneous requirements. You might, at that point, work with a third-party select-service manager like Crossroads Hospitality to take over your hotel and manage it for you. They manage it, help you grow it, and you pay them a fee.)

To take it to another level, if you own a Residence Inn, which is a select-service hotel under the Marriott brand, you could manage that hotel yourself, you could have Marriott manage it, or you could outsource it to a third party, like Crossroads Hospitality. This is what is meant by a third-party manager. Crossroads is like the secret weapon helping to make everything happen more effectively for a smaller hotel owner.

Sales Team Size and Job Description: There were four divisions of Crossroads nationwide, and in the beginning (2001) each division had a vice president of sales who was in charge of each region that managed approximately twenty-five hotels. Each hotel typically had only one sales professional responsible for helping to build the success of a particular location. Their job was to capture more market share, generate more revenue, and be a good brand steward.

Leadership Team Goal: The goal of the management team at Crossroads is to incentivize and inspire the sales team to gain market share from competitors in a measurable way and support the individual sales representatives in their efforts.

Because there is only one person in each location, they are fairly isolated versus working with a couple of people in a sales department (which typically happens in a larger hotel). This is not uncommon for many industries. They are small and siloed and they have to figure out how to be strong, effective, and scrappy and work autonomously because they don't always have access to one another. From a leadership standpoint, it can be hard to rally the troops when your people are spread out all over the country.

Challenge to Overcome: To maintain and build market share in a difficult economy. (The hospitality industry as a whole was affected significantly after the tragedy of 9/11.)

Strategy: To hold a special fourth-quarter sales competition to build up morale and drive sales to develop new business.

First Scrappy Contest/Sales Blitz: 2001 (with four divisions, approximately one hundred hotels, and 130 salespeople at the property level).

Final Scrappy Contest/Sales Blitz: 2011 (with four divisions, approximately two hundred hotels, and 250–260 salespeople at the property level).

Results: Crossroads Hospitality experienced a significant increase in sales and the creation of a vibrant culture where creativity and originality were valued. The company almost doubled in size in approximately ten years. The sharing of best practices among peers was the most significant game changer to the organization's growth.

This concept of getting scrappy and the sharing of best practices helped to build a strong and unique company culture, increase team effectiveness, increase market share, and increase individual and overall location production.

Here's the story:

Back in May 2001, I was invited to speak at the national sales meeting of Crossroads Hospitality on the topic of persuasive presentation skills. After my program, the leaders of the management team were inspired by a segment of my talk on the idea of getting scrappy, but they weren't entirely sure what to do with it or how to proceed.

The leaders knew they wanted to create a new corporate culture around the idea of maximizing creativity and sharing inventive ideas and best practices among employees across the division. In my interview with Tom, he shared how the whole concept of getting scrappy got started:

> I was on the flight home from that conference in May and sitting next to Leslie Freeman, the VP of sales and marketing at the time. We were discussing your speech and the segment specifically on the idea about getting scrappy. We asked, "What can we do with this?" and decided to focus a significant sales push for the fourth quarter around this idea. We took the word "scrappy" and broke it down into an acronym that fit our company mission, ultimately coming up with: Stealing Customers Rapidly Aggressively Passionately Persuasively Year-round. And that was it— that was the beginning. This may seem hard to believe, but from

that initial meeting, this is how everything got started and the entire shift of our company's culture began.

They were thinking through a lot of different ideas, and then there was a hard stop due to 9/11. After 9/11, the country was still reeling from terrorist attacks that had devastated the economy, particularly those sectors related to travel and hospitality industries. They had to keep things moving. Tom explains: "By October of 2001, we launched a special sales contest called the 'Crossroads Scrappy 100 National Sales Blitz.' It started with that first sales meeting and continued growing consistently and organically over the next ten years, concluding with the Scrappy 1000 in 2011."

The challenge was to encourage employees to come up with innovative ideas to generate new business with both existing and new accounts. They could earn points individually and as a team, and ultimately the people and regions with the most points at the end of the contest would win cash prizes.

The result? The short answer is it worked. The teams had fun and increased business and revenue, and the company gained new ground. They shared the ideas that worked and those that didn't, and it truly inspired an environment of fresh creativity. It also generated some fantastic collaboration and team building. By employing a new take on the traditional sales contest, Crossroads energized its employees and gained new ground at the same time.

The long answer is even better. When I began talking to Tom about Crossroads' scrappy effort, I was pleased to find how closely its plan unintentionally mirrored the three elements of getting scrappy that we discussed earlier, which parallel the DARPA model:

1. Crossroads laid out an audacious goal for itself: to spur a significant sales increase during the slowest time of the year.
2. It established a finite time line of ninety days (fourth quarter).
3. It gave employees the freedom they needed to execute their ideas.

Tom explained that taken individually, each of these elements might have generated noticeable gains for Crossroads. But it was the combination of all three that ignited creativity at every level and established a truly scrappy culture.

> I think the last one, [the freedom to execute], is probably the most important when you talk about those three things. . . . We, as leaders, just set the template. We set the stage. We created the incentives. We allowed them to build their own plan in order to customize for their specific markets, but the freedom was the key. Because if we had just told them what to do and how to do it, I don't think it would have taken off and become the DNA of our division.
>
> As of 2001, at the end of the year, if you got scrappy and produced during this blitz, not only could you win cash prizes, but you could potentially win a slot on a cruise. They worked toward their annual goals all year. The fourth quarter was the perfect time to run the sales blitz—during the slowest time of the year [for our business]. That fourth quarter gave us the time frame to be able to really drive a strong finish all the way down to the wire, and it drove competition. That's why the time frame was important and we kept to it.
>
> People would gear up for the blitz because over and over again if we produced the midyear numbers and posted the standings in June, it would always change by the fourth quarter because

somebody could come from behind and win. That was the excitement that kept it going.

Crossroads' scrappy culture developed over time and really took off after regional divisions began creating their own acronyms and giving themselves their own unique names. For instance, the northeast division was called BRATS, for Booking Revenue And Taking Share. That process helped build unity at the regional level, and as a result, the companywide competition gained momentum.

> *We had people really taunting each other via e-mail which was fantastic because they were like, "Look at what we did. We booked another hundred thousand!" The other group would come back and talk about it and there would be about five or six stories all combined in an e-mail. It was exciting to watch people going back and forth talking about this competition among the teams that were on a bigger scale versus one individual celebrating their own success at one hotel.*
>
> *As more individuals and regional teams acquired the scrappy mindset, it became a real differentiator for Crossroads as a whole. Because of the uniqueness of this culture, Crossroads made a name for itself. It literally became what the division was known for and it was quite exciting to watch it all develop and then just keep feeding it.*

Because that first sales blitz contest was a success, Crossroads decided to do it again the next year, calling it the Scrappy 200, and then again and again. They realized that getting scrappy as a movement was about more than achieving a one-time win. It was a spirited approach that would generate repeatable efforts as the company tried to acquire new business. Ultimately, Crossroads continued the fourth-quarter Scrappy National Sales Blitz Contest for more than ten years, ending with the Scrappy 1000 in 2011. It became a defining part of Crossroads' culture.

"As I moved from my role as vice president of sales to the president of the division, Denny Stewart became the VP and took things to the next level," Tom said. Notably, Crossroads Hospitality doubled its size from 2007 to 2011 and its growth is attributed to the evolution of its scrappy culture.

At this point, you might be thinking: "Okay, Crossroads energized its workforce and had a lot of fun, but what is the tangible evidence of that success?" During its decade of getting scrappy, the company measured its success in four different areas:

- Building a strong and unique company culture
- Increasing team effectiveness
- Increasing market share
- Increasing individual and overall production

Company Culture

Company culture speaks to the vision, values, norms, language, and beliefs of the organization. It is something that is preexisting in your company's genetic code; it's not something that employees bring with them. "Our company culture expanded under a scrappy philosophy. It set the tone for engagement in the field and the behavior that pulled things through," Tom said.

The members of the sales teams not only challenged themselves, they challenged one another. They would share their scrappy efforts on a regular basis, via e-mail and other platforms. Their ideas were clever, fun, nervy, and most of all inspiring. "It could be something that they did that was unique that allowed them to open a door that might never have been opened before . . . within our culture they had an opportunity to think differently."

The word "scrappy" eventually became synonymous with Crossroads. "When you talked about us, that's what you talked about—it was our scrappy sales culture," Tom said.

The culture was driven by the sales team as well as the mindset and the effort of the management. The following story from Tom illustrates how the sales managers contributed to the development of the company culture in a fun way:

> *Every year, at the end of the Scrappy Blitz, the competition was fierce between the different regional sales teams as they tried to win extra slots on the seven-day cruises. We set up a wild-card drawing to keep it interesting and exciting while points were tallied. The race to the finish line was always dramatic. One year it was a particularly tight race between all the regions, so I spontaneously put together a last-minute competition to break the tie. I announced there would be a swim-off where the regional directors of sales of each team had to swim the length of a pool. This came as a surprise to everyone, especially the regional directors. The rules were: there were no rules. They jumped in with their suits on, would hold on to each other's legs to get ahead of one another, and it was hilarious. It was even more exciting as the teams*

cheered their regional captain on! The energy was powerful and really contributed to the long-term scrappy culture we were trying to build.

The managers fought hard to win. Their efforts showed, and it was symbolic of getting into the trenches, getting into the fight with their teams and leading. "You should have seen the enthusiasm of the winning team when the winner crossed the finish line."

Team Effectiveness

Team effectiveness is the capacity a team has to accomplish the goals or objectives set forth by the leadership of an organization. It's critical to Crossroads as a company to consistently improve team effectiveness through tenure (retention of employees), staff unity, and stability in sales (which relates to consistency in maintenance of clients).

> *Stability in the sales force supports repeat customers. . . . When you keep somebody at a local level for three to five to ten years, they're going to book more business because people know them, they're effective, and they understand the marketplace. That consistency really helps because we secure people in locations who want to grow within the company and produce more for us in those market places long-term.*

As the scrappy efforts multiplied during the scrappy sales blitz period and even more employees were inspired to get creative, Tom found himself inundated with strategies that people were executing across the division. Here's an example of a tenured team that got scrappy and utilized their understanding of the needs of the local market to steal business from a competitor:

> *The Houston Texans football team had been staying at a full-service hotel and facility. It was a big seven-story high-rise build-ing. Our Residence Inn hotel team needed to get SCRAPPY if they were going to lure the Texans to leave the competitor and move to our exterior hotel with eight rooms per building (similar to how townhomes are set up).*
>
> *During a site visit with the client, the entire Residence Inn staff joined in the effort to capture their business. From the front desk to housekeeping, everyone was onboard: To show team spirit the staff all wore the Texans' team jersey. . . . Because safety and secu-rity was a critical issue in the client's decision-making process, the director of sales had a bold idea of building a one-arm gate and fence providing access to the team only in the back section of the hotel. . . . The bonus differentiator was kitchen access on-site for the team members. The Texans loved the fact that Residence Inn had full kitchens so players had a place to cook after long days of training camp. Out-of-the-box thinking helped the Residence Inn team tackle the Texans business and secure the contract.*

Market Share

Market share is a critical component from the client's perspective. Obviously Crossroads cares about market share because when it in-creases market share, the client is happy. When the client is happy, Crossroads is happy.

Crossroads helped its clients to develop an increase in market share that grew anywhere from 5 percent to 10 percent in varying amounts over a ten-year period. These are outstanding results.

By 2006, the division was celebrating its fifth contest, the Scrappy 500 National Sales Blitz, and a sales revenue increase of more than $2.5 million. The next year, in 2007, the Scrappy 600 National Sales Blitz generated a revenue increase of almost $1.5 million. Even during the economic downturn, Crossroads continued along its scrappy path, generating new and unique ideas, if not a revenue surge.

> *The SCRAPPY 400 produced $4 million, the SCRAPPY 500 $6.3 million, and the SCRAPPY 600 $8 million. This fourth-quarter production could either be consumed in the fourth quarter or potentially exist in the first quarter. That was the time frame that we needed it to be in because if we were gaining occupancy or average rate during those months, that meant we were gaining market share during the toughest time by stealing it from competitors.*

Individual and Overall Location Production

Individual production speaks to the amount of sales generated by an individual over a defined sales cycle, such as quarterly or annual individual sales production results. This is a measurable benchmark to assess growth for the sales team members separately. The energy of the scrappy culture significantly affected individual production at Crossroads. There was an increase in production on average of 10 percent per person on their individual goals during the fourth-quarter sales blitz consistently over that ten-year period, netting the individual producers prizes, income, trips, and the like.

THINGS TO CONSIDER

You may be wondering if there is any downside or any negative issues that need to be considered before promoting scrappiness within your organization. That depends on the organization. Tom highlighted the following three issues you may have to contend with:

1. Dealing with the skeptics
2. Managing inappropriate or over-the-top scrappy gestures and managing rogue employees
3. Finding and screening for scrappy talent

Dealing with the Skeptics

When the scrappy culture began to breathe new life into Crossroads' fourth quarter, which was typically the slowest time of the year, Tom was confronted with a few skeptics. They asked, "If the Scrappy Blitz is so effective, why don't we run it year-round? Why not transform the entire fiscal year?" Tom knew that removing the element of a limited time line from the mix would kill the sheer nature of what makes somebody *want* to get scrappy.

We avoided that like the plague. We didn't want to make this an everyday occurrence. If we had, it would have taken away the special sweet sauce that we knew was key. In the hospitality in-dustry, the fourth quarter drags behind all the others. There's less occupancy because there's less demand. In the fourth quarter, you need to get scrappy. Think about it: You have all of this supply that's not getting filled up, so you compress the time frame to really motivate people to increase their production and ultimately increase your market share. And you know what? It works. But you can't do it all year-round and think that it's going to continue to be sustainable. To remain worthy and special, the Scrappy Blitz had to be the exception, not the rule.

Managing Inappropriate or Over-the-Top Scrappy Gestures and Managing Rogue Employees

I asked Tom if he ever had to rein someone in. Did anybody go too far in a way that negatively affected the company? How were those missteps turned into teachable moments?

To ensure that ideas stayed within professional and ethical boundaries, the senior management at Crossroads monitored be-havior from a distance but made a point of giving the employees and teams the utmost freedom to experiment. "I really believe in the 'freedom to execute,' as you said, and allowing them to do what they wanted to do in their markets," Tom said.

First of all, as we would receive these stories at the main office, we filtered all the information before it was sent back out to the field. If we received something we thought was not in alignment with our culture, we would filter that and then write back to that individual and say, "This is a teaching moment. It is a learning opportunity," and those were really important. We didn't let the thing run wild. We had to define [the boundaries] occasionally with individuals who went a little "off the grid." So I think it was important that we controlled it. Even though we let the freedom exist, we controlled the messaging of it.

In terms of leadership, Tom's approach was a bit risky. He basically said, "All right, we're giving you permission to color outside the lines. Be professional, be ethical, and don't do anything that's against the law. Be respectful of people's time. As long as it's under these terms, you're free." His approach required trust in his employees but also demanded the highest level of professionalism.

It was all based on risk/reward, risk/reward. We knew that the risk could be there but we also knew the rewards would be significant. If we controlled the atmosphere and the environment of how to be successful and how to be scrappy, then how could it really happen? Think about the words "stealing customers." We were not looking to be passive. We really focused on what "persuasively" meant and how to communicate that.

While there are many examples of people who did something a little bit crazy (like following someone from a parking lot to their office space), there are many, many more stories of individuals doing random acts of kindness. It was these consistent acts of kindness, thoughtfulness, and creativity in terms of how they approached someone, how they maintained their relationship, how they went back and did something after the fact, that was memorable. We say the word "aggressively" when we're talking about the acronym, but they were aggressively kind and also had a sense of urgency in their efforts. The day-to-day blocking and tackling of getting appointments, finally connecting with prospects, and getting meetings that you couldn't get for six months because they wouldn't call you back . . . those were celebrated just as much as the bookings and the results in terms of closing deals because we wanted to emphasize that it doesn't always lead to a booking right away. It might lead to the next opportunity.

Finding and Screening for Scrappy Talent

Even if you like the idea of getting scrappy within your organization, you may be concerned about dealing with employees or associates who will not be all that thrilled to jump aboard the scrappy train. I made a point of asking Tom about push-back, and his insight makes perfect sense when you consider what a powerful environment a scrappy culture can be:

It's challenging to find sales professionals with a scrappy mindset. . . . So we tried our best to cultivate that trait early in the onboarding process. I think new recruits realized they were not going to be able to last long in the company if they didn't adopt a scrappy attitude. There was a tribal effect. . . . It almost felt like the majority ruled and this is what it's going to be.

In fact, the scrappy mindset was so deeply ingrained in the Crossroads division that managers began to screen for it during hiring assessments, often asking candidates to share the ways they had stolen market share or generated new business in a creative way. "It was part of our mindset and everybody was in on it. The whole company realized that if you were attached to this division, that's what it was going to take," Tom said.

HOW DO YOU GET STARTED WITHIN YOUR ORGANIZATION? START SMALL

After reading the Crossroads story, you might be inspired to do the same with your company. So how do you get started? The answer is to start small. Try to use getting "scrappy" as a theme for an upcoming conference or retreat. See if it takes and gradually share the ideas with more and more of your organization. Be patient because it takes time. Crossroads Hospitality/Interstate Hotels & Resorts didn't come up with their ideas overnight. They were stimulated by an initial idea and expanded each year until the scrappy culture grew organically into the fabric of the company. The leaders who achieve this shift are those who are willing to get in the game with their employees, foster an environment of creative freedom, and recruit talent that thrives in a scrappy culture.

As this mini case study shows us, a company's wide-scale scrappy effort is only as strong and as deep as its leaders' vision. Still, getting scrappy is a daunting task—whether you are an individual looking to change her circumstances, a small business owner, or a member of a large team of sales professionals. The best preparation for your scrappy effort includes time set aside to study the efforts of others.

AN AWARD TO CHERISH: CROWNED THE KING OF SCRAPPINESS

By 2015 on his departure from the company, Tom Bardenett was known as "Mr. Scrappy" among his colleagues. They even gave him an award—a trophy customized with the varying themes of the Scrappy Blitz competitions over the years—and crowned him the King of Scrappiness.

It may not be the most attractive award I've ever received, but it's the one that means the most to me. It cracks me up and

*represents the amazing team and the wonderful people with whom
I had the pleasure of working.*

So what's the key to Crossroads' scrappy success? "Give people the flexibility and adaptability to be creative. Let them enjoy that. . . . That's where the power is."

Tom has since moved on to lead another organization, so I asked him: "Is 'getting scrappy' part of your new leadership strategy?" His answer: "Absolutely! And it's already started. . . ."

REVIEW

- The common denominator between companies and organizations that successfully foster a scrappy culture is leadership.
- Scrappy leaders:
  - Are willing to get their hands dirty and literally get in the game with the team. They employ scrappy efforts themselves.
  - Foster an environment of creative freedom to execute ideas.
  - Recruit, cultivate, and support talent that thrives in a scrappy environment.
  - Nurture and develop what others might consider "rogue" talent.
- Case Study—How Crossroads Hospitality took the idea of getting scrappy and scaled it within their organization to build a highly effective culture:
  - This concept of getting scrappy and the sharing of best practices helped to build a strong and unique company culture,

increase team effectiveness, increase market share, and increase individual and overall location production.

- Three things to consider before promoting scrappiness within your organization:
  - Dealing with the skeptics
  - Managing inappropriate or over-the-top scrappy gestures and managing rogue employees
  - Finding and screening for scrappy talent

What's Next: Random elements: the X Factor and leaving room for serendipity.

Chapter 9

LEAVING ROOM
FOR SERENDIPITY

IT'S IMPORTANT TO NOTE THAT THERE ARE OFTEN UNPRE-
dictable aspects to getting scrappy, specifically the X Factor and serendipity. There are no guarantees when getting scrappy. The main
thing to remember when you execute a strategy is to stay flexible in
the face of life's twists and turns.

RANDOM ELEMENTS: THE X FACTOR
AND SERENDIPITY

The success of your scrappy effort depends on several different factors. Every scrappy strategy is the sum of a large number of moving
parts. Many are within your control, but some are not.

Enter the X Factor.

When it comes to getting scrappy, the magic is in the mix.
There's always the X Factor that can change the game entirely. It is

a circumstance, quality, or person that has a strong but unpredictable influence on the outcome of an event. Call it luck, timing, or preparedness. Call it a blessing or being in the zone. It's an event or sequence of events that seems perfectly unbelievable.

The X Factor is beautifully illustrated in the story of Debby Carreau. Born in South Africa, she now resides in Canada and is the CEO and founder of Inspired HR, Ltd., a Canadian consulting firm that manages human resources for more than 300,000 employees across North America. In her early years as a college student, Debby worked part time in a restaurant and fell in love with the hospitality industry and its people. She had a flair for the work and began landing promotions that eventually placed her at the management level. "When I was twenty-three years old, I was given what was essentially the chance of a lifetime. I was offered the opportunity to buy into and become the managing partner of a high-volume Milestones restaurant flagship location in downtown Vancouver."

What were the odds? Milestones was a major company and part of the highly successful Spectra Group of Great Restaurants. Sure, many of us in our early twenties worked in restaurants to get through college, but how many of us were given the opportunity to *buy into* those restaurants as an owner? Clearly there was something about Debby's passion and work ethic that sparked Milestones' attention. The two gentlemen who owned the restaurant were particularly impressed with Debby's leadership skills and her ability to groom others for success. For Debby, the offer was staggering in scope. She *really* wanted to do it!

The challenge was that she didn't have the money, and she

didn't feel she could ask any family or friends for help. Just thinking about the amount she needed was overwhelming. But she didn't let that stop her. Throwing in the towel didn't even cross her mind. She forged ahead, convinced she could find a solution.

> *Looking back, I can see how naïve I was. It was exciting and flattering, and it happened so quickly that I didn't know what I didn't know. I just knew it was one of those pivotal moments, and I think Sheryl Sandberg said it best: "If you're offered a seat on a rocket ship, you take the seat and figure out the details later."*
>
> *Right off the bat, I figured my best option was to go to a bank. That's where the money is, so that's what I did. And I acted quickly because I felt like it was a now-or-never opportunity. I literally drove to the local branch of my bank, without an appointment, and asked to speak to the manager, a wonderful man named Doug, who's now retired. I told him about the offer, jotted down a few numbers, and explained that I didn't have any kind of formal business plan. Fortunately, the restaurant group was a well-known brand with a high-volume business, and Doug approved my loan.*

Once again, Debby defied the odds. With no collateral, a minimal credit history, and a huge dose of excitement, confidence, and earnest ambition, she landed the seed money she needed to buy into the project.

Debby secured the loan in a short amount of time—about thirty days after getting the offer—which means she didn't spend a lot of time waffling or seeking advice from other people. That was on purpose. Her parents were financially conservative and most likely would have talked her out of taking such a risk. So she kept her plan to herself.

Luckily, it was one of the best financial decisions I've ever made. Looking back, I'm glad I wasn't risk averse and that it turned out well. I certainly never dreamed I'd be making north of six figures at twenty-three years old. It really helped my confidence and I found myself saying, "If I can do this, what else can I do? What's next?"

In fact, buying into that first restaurant led to a second restaurant and eventually served as a springboard to Debby's current career in human resources. When Spectra Group was bought out by an even larger company, she was tapped to head its human resources division. That opportunity positioned her to start her own firm, Inspired HR.

Both the restaurant executives and the local bank manager recognized Debby's potential as a good investment. After all, there was no logic in asking a twenty-three-year-old restaurant manager to be a partner in a major deal or giving that same young woman a huge loan for a business plan that wasn't even down on paper. But it happened, and the X Factor applies here. Somewhere along the way, they just decided that Debby was a good bet.

You just never know when the X Factor might come into play. It can be that special something that gives you a "miracle-like" opportunity when you least expect it.

Curveballs and Serendipity

One of the best moments in life is looking back and realizing how much better things turned out because your plan didn't go exactly as planned. Have you ever had a situation shift in a way that you couldn't possibly have anticipated? We all have. It's just part of life's adventure. Even after the best planning, preparation, and research, you can still get thrown a curveball. You might think it's the end of the world— but is it? Have you ever said to yourself: "Wait, what just happened? We didn't plan for that!" Then, out of nowhere, what you thought was something negative turns out to be a positive, and ultimately, the outcome is better than you could have planned for or even imagined.

There might be an occasion when your scrappy effort looks and feels like it has failed, but you are actually on a path to an extraordinary opportunity. Family wealth counselor Ken Fink has experienced this particular kind of good fortune firsthand. A few years ago, a friend of his referred him to a prospective client—let's call him Alan—who lived in Cleveland, Ohio. Alan was a successful real estate developer with a high net worth who seemed well suited for Ken's services. Completing his usual due diligence and research, Ken spoke with Alan via telephone, arranged an appointment, booked an airplane ticket, and flew to Cleveland. He arrived at Alan's office building fifteen minutes early, but it turned out Alan wasn't there and no one seemed to even know that Ken had an appointment with him. The meeting was a complete bust, and Ken wasn't quite sure what to do. Should he go get coffee? Return to the airport? Or just hang around the lobby of Alan's office building and hope he shows up?

Then Ken remembered it was April 15, tax return day in the United States, and just a couple of buildings away on the same street was a CPA firm he was working with on another matter. He decided to pop in and say hello to his buddy Jeff. Unfortunately, Jeff was slammed with clients anxious to file their tax returns and he could only spare a minute.

> As I'm talking to Jeff, I heard a voice coming from behind me, down the hall. Somebody asked, "Are you a rabbi?"
>
> I wear a yamaka because I'm an Orthodox Jew, so I turned around, and I saw an elderly gentleman standing there. I was sort of shocked by the question, and I said, "No, I'm actually a family wealth counselor."
>
> The elderly man said, "What the hell is that?" in an inquisitive tone.
>
> I thought about it for a second and said, "Well, I'm kind of a Jewish Robin Hood. I take taxes from the government and give to charity."
>
> He said, "I have no idea what that means!" Then he added, "When you're done here, come on downstairs to my office."

Not sure what to think, Ken immediately turned to Jeff, who informed him the elderly gentleman was a bit eccentric but owned the building they were standing in and several others on the same street. He urged Ken to get down to the man's office as soon as possible.

> I finished up my business with Jeff very quickly and I went downstairs. I'm not exaggerating when I say that I sat down at

the elderly gentleman's desk and he puts in front of me his net worth statement within ten minutes of our conversation. He said to me, "Can you do something about these taxes?"

I was looking at the financial statement and I saw that it read something about $200 million in assets! And I'm thinking, "Is there an extra zero on this thing?"

Ken calmly advised the older man that he could help solve his problem with a variety of strategies, including a family retreat process paired with the elimination of taxes and the creation of charitable benefits. "He was intrigued, and to make a long story short, that led to doing a family retreat for this gentleman which led to the evolution of one of the most important and largest relationships of my career. . . . It really ended up helping us turn the corner for our business nationally as well. . . ."

So Ken's missed meeting with Alan led him down a path to a business owner who would become one of his favorite and most loyal clients. That chance meeting evolved into an unbelievable relationship that continues to thrive eighteen years later. What a gift that "Alan" was a no-show or this never would have happened. "He has introduced us to many people and we've done many wonderful things together. So, you know, we just never know where something's gonna go. We start at point A and could end up at point Z. One never knows!"

That's the beauty of serendipity. It's the good fortune of finding valuable or pleasant things that you didn't expect and were not looking for. Ken's story is a beautiful illustration of serendipity because he just stayed the course even when it took him in a direction that didn't look promising. He could have given up. He could have chosen to sit in the Cleveland airport all afternoon with a bad attitude. But he didn't. He kept an open mind and a scrappy attitude. He tried to make the best use of his time under the circumstances and it paid off.

Allow room for serendipity. I like to think it's similar to when you realize you've gone in the wrong direction or taken the wrong turn while driving a car. Your GPS "recalculates" and puts you back on course, maybe in a better way. But in any case, you have to be willing to follow the new directions and trust it will get you to where you want to go eventually.

Also, watch for the signs. Don't limit your options with old beliefs and your negative forecasting; you don't know how the journey will end or how things will unfold. "Trust the force, young Skywalker!"

It's important to accept that sometimes your scrappy effort is not going to work. But keep your eyes and your heart open for the unexpected. Along the journey there are cool little things that happen that we dismiss as insignificant, but then you turn a corner and that "little thing" leads you to an amazing opportunity or introduction.

Accept these realities:

1. Sometimes something happens right away.
2. Sometimes something happens in a couple of weeks.
3. Sometimes something happens in a few years.

It's that simple. I bet if you pause for a moment and reflect on the experiences that brought you to where you are today, you can relate to what I'm talking about here.

REVIEW

- There are no guarantees when getting scrappy. The most important thing is to stay flexible in the face of life's twists and turns.
- The X Factor can change the game entirely. It is a circumstance, quality, or person that has a strong but unpredictable influence on the outcome of an event.
- There might be an occasion when your scrappy effort looks and feels like it has failed, but you are actually on a path to an extraordinary opportunity. That's the beauty of serendipity. It's the good fortune of finding valuable or pleasant things that you didn't expect and were not looking for.

What's Next: It's time to execute your plan and put your tush on the line. Let's review the Scrappy Strategy Action Plan Checklist.

Getting in the Ring—
Bonus Scrappy Success Story #5
ON SECOND CHANCES

SOMETIMES WE GET THE WIN WE'VE BEEN WORKING TOWARD, but then the outcome doesn't go the way we had hoped. Your project might be terminated because it loses funding. Or you're downsized. Maybe you find yourself shut out, or simply dismissed. It's a discouraging place to be. What do you do if your pet project or dream job is eliminated?

An amazing example of a scrappy response to such dire circumstances is the story of Paulo Coelho, a virtually unknown Brazilian author who penned *The Alchemist* in 1988. Paulo loved the story he'd written about a young shepherd in search of his treasure. Filled with strong spiritual overtones, it could, he firmly believed, be a success. Unfortunately, the book was initially a commercial failure. It simply didn't sell, and Paulo's first publisher dropped it. In the face of insurmountable odds, he refused to give up on this book or his writing career. Today, *The Alchemist* is renowned across the world. It has sold over 65 million copies and has been on *The New York Times* best seller list for more than 315 weeks. It's been translated into eighty different languages, setting the Guinness World Record for the most translated book by any living author.

In the fall of 2014, Paulo appeared on Oprah Winfrey's *Super Soul Sunday* and explained his book's unlikely journey and how it changed his life. He revealed that after being dropped by his publisher, he decided to try again to get it published. He even resolved to knock on doors to appeal to strangers to make that happen. "The first door that I knocked on, the guy opened. A very important publishing house in Brazil . . . And I said, 'I have a book that was published and did not sell. But I trust this book is going to sell. The guy said, 'Okay, I'm going to publish it.'"

With that one answer, he got a second chance. It seems unreal that once he decided to go ahead and knock on doors he got a deal so quickly. Or that he got a deal at all. That's unbelievable! That's not a common result. The X Factor is the only possible explanation we can apply to this particular scrappy story. It's important to reference that things have changed significantly in today's marketplace and that Paulo's ability to access the decision maker directly most likely wouldn't happen in the same way in today's market.

But what if it could be just that easy? Maybe it will be. You won't know until you try.

Chapter 10

EXECUTE YOUR PLAN: PUT YOUR TUSH ON THE LINE

Vision without action is daydream. Action without vision is nightmare.

—Japanese Proverb

THIS CHAPTER IS ABOUT PUTTING IT ALL TOGETHER AND WILL assist you in moving from the development and planning phase to the "go" phase. It's important to take action but only when you're ready. However, some people spend so much time getting ready that they never take action. If you want your circumstances to change, you have to stop tinkering and launch. Let's review a practical checklist to keep you on track and examine a few unique stories to help you get a clear picture of what "taking action" looks like as you move forward.

ON EXECUTION

At the point when you are ready to take action, that moment you are ready to execute, there might still be a wave or feeling of reluctance to "go," even if you have done your homework, anticipated failure, and sharpened your skills. Those feelings are normal. Your best defense, at that point, is to heed the wisdom of Amelia Earhart, who said, "The most effective way to do it . . . is to *do it!*"

It might be easier to begin thinking of your first scrappy effort as an experiment. Designating a venture as an experiment often lessens the pressure and conveys a feeling of minimal risk. It seems less like a pass-fail exam or a sink-or-swim feat and more like exploring a curiosity. In time, you can advance your scrappy effort to a level that involves more importance, more significance and more risk.

To dig a little deeper into the subject of execution and how it relates to getting scrappy, I visited with university director and leadership consultant Nick Lacy, who studies the cycle of execution and the pivotal role it plays in leadership development. In our conversation, we discussed key areas of execution worth considering when preparing to move forward: decision points, experimentation, and conviction.

Along your journey, there will be starts and stops and pivotal moments where you may pause and reflect—trying to decide the next best move. Nick calls these situations "decision points" and suggests, "You can ask yourself this clarifying question: If I do not do this, if I do not take this step, will I regret it? Or, in simple terms, which will feel worse: going for it or walking away?"

These decision points are important to contemplate. They will guide you when *choosing* what you need and want to do next.

In his research on execution, Nick has found that the reasons behind taking action vary depending on whether a person is executing an experiment or trying to move forward a conviction. There is a distinct difference between the two. "Executing an experiment is about self-discovery and learning what you believe is important in your life. Executing from a place of conviction is the result of a deep devotion to something."

For instance, Beck Bamberger executed an experiment when she committed to a year of uncomfortable experiences to push her own boundaries. On the other hand, Steven Schussler transformed his home into a jungle out of a deep devotion to his dream of creating a rain forest–themed restaurant. Both Beck and Steven had valid reasons to get scrappy and execute, but their strategies involved vastly different levels of intensity and risk.

Nick's research suggests that both motivations—experimentation and conviction—can build on each other to reveal the path ahead. Perhaps you have always wanted an entirely different job, so as an experiment, you apply for an internship—just ten hours a week—to get a taste of this new field. After several months (Decision Point!), you might discover you really love the industry and commit to a career change (Conviction!) or discover that, nope (Experiment Over!), that kind of work isn't for you.

Whatever the result, it's okay. The key is *executing* a strategy to find the answer. So whether you're driven by experimentation or a deep conviction, remember that no ground can be gained unless you follow through. Regardless of the reasons pushing you to act, it's time to implement your scrappy strategy. Carry out your plan and see what happens!

THE SCRAPPY STRATEGY ACTION PLAN CHECKLIST

We have already established that there is no specific recipe or exact formula for success when it comes to getting scrappy, but that doesn't mean you can't learn from those who have gone before you. In fact, you would be foolish not to. The stories in this book are invaluable, serving as informal yet true-to-life examples filled with best practices, if you will, for getting scrappy.

To that end, here's what I like to call the Scrappy Strategy Action Plan Checklist:

- ❑ Make the decision to play big and commit—decide to go!
- ❑ Set your goal.
- ❑ Identify the recipient: Whom do you need to influence to get where you want to go?
- ❑ Determine the best time to execute and invest in doing your research and homework.
- ❑ Start brainstorming and assemble your support team.
- ❑ Develop your plan: a Plan A and a Plan B.
- ❑ Conduct a premortem.
- ❑ Take action.

Remember: The process is fluid. Think back to our surfing analogy. When you're getting scrappy, you have to go with the flow. Like a wave, a scrappy effort really has a life of its own. It has its own energy and sometimes the wind will take you in directions you have not anticipated. Sometimes you start small and nothing really happens, so you increase the level of intensity. Next you try a medium-size effort and that doesn't really land either, so you try something bigger. It's progressive. But ultimately, the point of providing you with a checklist is to give you guidance so that you can plan appropriately and have a higher probability of a positive outcome in your execution.

What Does Taking Action Look Like?

Stories about effectively executing a scrappy effort are interesting and show us a behind-the-scenes look at what "taking action" really looks like. It can unfold in countless ways. It's like a metaphorical bout in the boxing ring, with a scrappy individual going up against a strong, fast, and experienced opponent. The following three illustrations provide insight into the personal experiences of scrappers from their perspectives. Each story demonstrates how a scrappy mindset, the freedom to execute, and a solid effort blend together to help obtain beautiful outcomes.

Damion Hickman Design vs. Quiksilver: Keep Showing Up,
Keep Doing the Work, and Stay the Course

Woody Allen was noted to have said that 80 percent of life is simply showing up. Though I can't pin it down to a firm number, that same thing is true about being scrappy. A huge part of giving yourself an edge is *showing up*, being prepared to dazzle a prospect or difficult listener, and doing the work—repeatedly, if necessary. It's about staying the course when others might quit. It's the moment when your mindset, your goal, and your research coalesce into one finely tuned scrappy effort. For my friend graphic designer Damion Hickman, this was the key to landing a dream account for his fledgling business. Here's his story:

It was early in my career as a graphic designer, I had started my own business and I was also working for a small label printer in Costa Mesa, California. At the end of the street where the printer company was based was a huge building where Quiksilver was located. I stared at it every day, and driving into work I would think, "Boy, it sure would be cool to do some surf designs for them." I pretty much would have done anything to get a chance at that.

After a couple of months of staring at the building, I decided to give it a shot. I walked over during one of my lunch breaks, met the receptionist, and asked her how I could go about getting some freelance work. She mentioned a particular fellow to talk with but he was unavailable. I left my name and phone number, and she politely agreed to give him my information.

Obviously this was pre-Internet and pre–cell phone, so I waited, pretty impatiently, for a phone call. No phone call came, so I went back a couple of days later. The receptionist said, "Well, you know what, I gave him the message. I'll give him the message again." We kept this up for a few weeks, with me dropping by every couple of days. We'd chat for a few minutes, and she'd promise to leave another message.

Finally, one day during one of my visits, I happen to see a guy walking down the stairs into the lobby just as I walk in. The receptionist said, "Oh hi, Damion," because by that point she knew me by name, and she kind of looked up at the guy walking down the stairs. (To respect his privacy I'll call him Joe for the purposes of the story.)

I seized the moment, walked over, and said, "Are you Joe?"

He said, "Yeah, are you Damion?" I said yes and he said, "Okay, I'll meet with you." On the inside, I was freaking out because I'd been trying for so long to land a meeting and suddenly it was go time! We walk into a conference room and he asks a few questions about my background before giving me a Quiksilver logo and telling me to come back with a few designs.

I was in! I went home, fired up my new computer and poured all of my free time (when I wasn't working at the print shop) into at least ten different designs for Quiksilver. In a few days, I went back in, and I was pretty pumped because Joe had said he'd pay $300 for each design. I thought, "Sweet, I'm making three grand today!" So we head to the conference room where Joe takes my designs and lays them all out on this giant table. I remember he had his hand over his mouth like he was thinking really hard and he starts flipping over the prints, one by one.

"Definitely not this one," he said. "Not this one." He flips over a few more until there's only one left. "Okay, here's what I want you to do to this one," he said, giving me some specific instructions. I asked if he wanted me to work on any of the other designs and he said, "No, just this one."

I go home, make the changes and head back the next day. "Okay, now make the font bigger," Joe said. I enlarge the font, get everything just right, and return to Joe's office where he said, "Okay, you know what, go ahead and change the colors on this part, make this part a bit larger, and make this part a lot smaller."

This back-and-forth went on for several days, and I eventually realized, "Oh, my gosh, I'm not getting $3,000. I'm getting only $300 for all of this work!" I wanted to quit, but I was determined to give him a design that he liked. I just told myself, "I'm going to come up with something that works—I don't care if I have to go a hundred rounds."

Finally, I go back to Joe's office, and I'm just desperate to get him to approve something. He looks at the design in my hand, crumples it up, and throws it in the garbage can. I can't believe it, and I sit there staring at him like, "What's going on?"

He just looked at me and said, "Okay, now let me give you a real assignment. I'm going to have you work on this, this, and this."

But I kept looking at the one in the garbage, the one I'd spent hours perfecting, and I asked, "What about that one?"

He said, "Oh, we're not using that. I'll pay you, of course, but I just wanted to see if you were going to stick it out, pay your dues, and do the work." I was floored. It was a little defeating, but I learned a lot from that. . . . Joe later shared that hardly any freelancers passed this test. After one or two rounds, he normally doesn't even hear from them again. I was twenty years old, and the bottom line is, I was just stoked to have the opportunity to do something for Quiksilver and they were one of my first real clients!

In fact, Damion's company, Damion Hickman Design, ended up landing multiple projects with Quiksilver as a result of that scrappy effort.

Over the years, I've realized that you have to be good at what you do, but you don't have to be the absolute best in the world to be really successful. A good chunk of our clients really appreciate the extra effort that our team gives. I've been known to take phone calls at ten o'clock at night, come in on the weekends, or drive stuff to a trade show in Las Vegas, Nevada, just because the customer needed it, and I really think that's why we still have a lot of our customers today.

What I love about Damion's story is its simplicity. He simply kept showing up and then backed up that effort with solid talent. He also exhibited patience. Sometimes a scrappy effort brings fast results, but other times you can find yourself playing a longer game—and that's okay.

Moral of the story: Keep showing up, keep doing the work, and stay the course when others might quit.

Steven Varela vs. Wizards of the Coast: Getting Scrappy Might Lead to a Success You Never Considered

Consider the following example my administrative marketing assistant Katelyn found online about a young man named Steven Varela who was applying for a new job as a gaming designer at Wizards of the Coast. What makes this story interesting is that he was already a Disney Imagineer (and by all accounts Steven already had an impressive résumé), but he still knew he needed to get scrappy to stand out from the competition in order to secure a new position with the gaming company.

Wizards of the Coast (often referred to as WotC or simply Wizards) is an American publisher of games (such as Magic: The Gathering and Dungeons & Dragons), primarily based on fantasy and science-fiction themes. Steven is an avid Dungeons & Dragons player and would get together weekly with friends from DreamWorks and Imagineering to play elaborate versions of the game in a home setting. Their version was more than just throwing dice on the table—Steven added props, had sound effects, and was adding control of the lighting into the rooms for special effects purposes. They actually had sessions where people would come just to watch them play.

In a blog post, Steven chronicles his supremely scrappy efforts to design, build, and deliver an elaborate and customized résumé to apply at WotC. We were so impressed by his story that we reached out to him directly to get the details.

I really got to flex my creative muscles with Walt Disney Imagineering and I genuinely enjoyed it . . . but I also wanted to look at new opportunities as I considered moving out of L.A. Upon the recommendation of a friend who knew someone at Wizards of the Coast and had spoken to this individual about my background and our D&D games, I decided to apply.

I was at my desk, ready to e-mail my résumé, and just as I was about to hit send, I stopped. I sat back and thought about it . . . I didn't believe they were going to look at my résumé as it was for

*more than five seconds before they chucked it in the trash—simply
because my experience with Disney is so different from the industry they're in.*

At that moment, he was "all in" to get scrappy and submit a résumé that would dazzle the CEO at Wizards of the Coast.

Steven's goal was to work in experimental game design for
WotC, so he knew he needed to showcase his ability to spin a compelling tale.

*I'm really passionate about storytelling, but I couldn't just
add this as a line on a résumé and have it be taken seriously. "I
am good at storytelling" does not translate!*

So one night, during one of his weekly Dungeons & Dragons
sessions with friends from Disney and DreamWorks, he figured
it out.

*I sat around the table thinking about it while we were actually
playing the game and I don't remember how I came up with it,
but I presented an idea to my group, and everybody kind of went
dead silent. Then they looked at me and they said, "If you don't
make this happen, we're going to be ashamed of you."*

During the next several days, he dug deep, focusing all of his
creative energy on crafting a story that Wizards of the Coast would
appreciate. "I kept building on the idea that I had this summoning
tablet," he said. By the end of the project, Steven had encased his

cover letter and résumé—both printed on handmade parchment to look sufficiently ancient—inside two intricately handcrafted and 3D-printed "gold" and "marble" tablets.

On one side of the tablets were the words "Whosoever shatters this tablet will have the ability to summon a powerful ally; but be warned, doing so will change the future, forever." On the other side were glyphs depicting what would happen once the tablets were shattered. But Steven didn't stop there. He really thought things through and anticipated how his résumé would, quite literally, be received—who might open it first and where it would be sent after that.

> *I knew I needed to have two tablets. I expected that whoever cracks the first tablet open will be so surprised by what happened that they will go tell everyone about what they just experienced . . . but they will only have a handful of shattered fragments and some paper to show their coworkers. The second tablet is the one that really matters. It will be the one that is delivered to the desk of the hiring manager who really needs to see it.*

Along the way, Steven's peers began to wonder if he was investing too much time and too many resources on what was essentially a gamble. "A lot of my friends came to me and actually said, 'Do you think this might be too much?' And I said to them, 'I won't know what the ceiling is until I hit it.'" For Steven, this was a mission of taking risks to showcase his skills, competency, and new perspectives.

So he kept going, customizing down to the last tiny detail so his message would resonate with the creative decision makers at Wizards of the Coast. When the tablets were finally completed, Steven sealed his résumés inside and packed them up. "I needed a container that furthered the story behind these tablets," he said. "Inspired by a bunch of different films, I made it look like an old museum artifact crate. I actually went to an equestrian center to get fresh hay and straw to use as a packing material." When he carried it into the UPS Store to ship it, he found out it weighed seventy pounds.

> *It was awesome, and everybody was asking me, "What's in the crate? What's in the crate?" And right there, that was when I started to get really excited because they were intrigued even without being part of the target audience. It was kind of a little flag that said I was heading in the right direction!*

Steven shipped the crate directly to Greg Leeds, the CEO of Wizards of the Coast. "I had tracking on it, so I could see where it was going step by step, and I'm telling you, time just slowed down once it arrived!" he said. "I was sitting there waiting, waiting!" About twenty-four hours after the crate was delivered, Steven received a personal e-mail from Greg Leeds.

> *The e-mail basically said, "This was the most fantastic résumé I have ever seen and it really speaks to your skill sets and your ambitions." Unfortunately, they said they were in a hiring downswing. They were not seeking to expand in that particular area. However, they were so impressed with the quality of my*

résumé and the delivery—that they asked if they could send out my contact information to a number of other parties that do vendor work for them. So that itself, a recommendation from a CEO at Wizards of the Coast, carries its weight in gold!

And it was through that connection that Steven ended up finding a new job with a Seattle-based company to help it develop interactive museum exhibit designs. Steven notes that this new company wasn't even on his radar as an opportunity, but it turned out to be the next-phase dream job in his career.

I asked Steven if he was ever nervous about executing his elaborate plan, and his answer revealed a beautiful mix of experiment and conviction:

> *The only thing I was really anxious about was inaction at that point. . . . I didn't feel that this was, in any way, a losing situation. I'd still gain some incredible experience. And the only thing I could have done to hurt myself was not act. I actually believe I gained more confidence as my project gained momentum. Soon, it was carrying me. . . . Even if I didn't get the job, I knew I would still learn something that was immensely valuable moving forward.*

Clearly this was a very elaborate effort to deliver a résumé in a highly competitive situation. Steven spent a great deal of time, energy, effort, and money (about $300) to put together his scrappy strategy to stand out from other applicants.

Remember, your scrappy action isn't typically going to be a

one-time, end-all-be-all effort. Sometimes it twists and turns and morphs along the way. It's the action you take to get to the next best step in earning you the right to be heard, seen, or noticed. It's your well-crafted strategy to sell yourself, to reach your goal, and to finally hear a yes.

Moral of the story: Getting scrappy might lead to a success you never considered. Instead of reaching your original goal, you might discover an even better opportunity.

Erik Sherman vs. Katie Couric: Find Workarounds and Stay the Course, and Things Can Turn Out Exactly as You Hoped

This is the story of Lehigh University student Erik Sherman and his classmates and their quest to persuade broadcast journalist Katie Couric to speak at their graduation ceremony.

It was 1999 and I was the vice president of my graduating class at Lehigh University, and one of the responsibilities of the class officers was to select a speaker for the commencement ceremony. So we set our sights on Katie Couric and decided to kind of "go to work" in terms of engaging her in a conversation to come and be our speaker. (The university really left it in our hands to kind of figure out and formulate a plan of how we were going to do this.) Of course, at that time, Katie Couric was certainly at the top of her game and we quickly learned that it was very difficult to just get through not one, but many layers of gatekeepers. We sent letters. We sent flowers. We called and left many messages with many different people. Finally, the president of our university told us we needed to seriously consider moving on to a different candidate. He was right. At this point we had been at it for about three months. But we did not like our other options as much and we certainly were not putting enough time and attention into securing them. His sense of urgency only made us think harder and more creatively about what could be done to at least get a response from Katie Couric.

One evening I was speaking with my dad, and I filled him in on our progress—or lack thereof. He asked if he could help, and me being who I am, I said, "I appreciate the offer, but I don't think we need your help at this point in time."

Not knowing anything about how my dad could possibly help, I just thought he was being that fatherly figure who was trying to support you and say, "Let me know if there's something I can do." And that was the extent of that conversation.

About a week later the president of the university insisted that we pursue a different candidate and even started lining up our second and third choices. I didn't want to quit. I knew I needed to do something . . . so I called my dad and humbly asked for help. It turned out one of his colleagues knew Katie Couric personally, and he agreed to ask this woman if she would pass along to Couric a personal invite to be our commencement speaker. It was our first break! (I probably should have listened to him and accepted his help much earlier.)

We crafted the most sincere invitation we could, with the best message and heartfelt, passionate wording and delivered it to my dad. He gave it to his colleague, who promised to personally give it to Couric herself. A few days later we received a personal note from her in which she politely declined our invitation. At this point, the president of the university urged us to get moving on other candidates. (But I was not giving up—I was all in. As you would say, time to get scrappy!) I told him to give us twenty-four hours. I figured, "Hey, she knows about us and she responded, so we are going to get in our cars at three a.m. tomorrow morning, drive down to the Today show, and stand outside the window set with signs and big smiles." And we did. We stood there with signs that simply said, "Lehigh wants Katie Couric to be our commencement graduation speaker!"

During a commercial break, Couric was courteous enough to come over and speak to us. I think her words were, "You guys aren't giving up!"

And we simply said, "Look, we really believe you are the right person for this. We truly want you to be our commencement speaker." She was touched by how far we had come, and how persistent we were being. But she said that twelve other schools had made the same request and she didn't think she could choose one over the other. We quickly pointed out that none of those schools had pursued her the way we had.

So she said, "Look, Erik, give me a call on Monday." (This was a Friday!) She didn't say yes, but she did give us an opportunity to engage in a real conversation or dialogue over the phone rather than through the mail.

I did call, of course, and only had to get past two gatekeepers before actually speaking with Katie Couric. She said she was willing to consider making the speech and wanted to know the date of our graduation. After I told her the date, she realized she had another engagement that night and seemed truly disappointed. The problem, she said, was that she would have to be back at home in Connecticut that same night.

Still not willing to give up, I asked her to give me twenty-four hours to see if I could come up with a solution. I had no idea what kind of solution I was going to come up with. All I knew was that she had more or less said yes to speaking at our commencement address, but the date didn't work and I had to fix it.

I had no ideas. You can't just find a speaker with a couple of months left to go. People have calendars, they have itineraries, they have other engagements you've got to work around. You can't just move a graduation date to accommodate someone else's schedule. It's set in stone.

So I called the president of the university (who by this time was losing patience with me) and asked for a favor. Not a little favor—a big favor. We go marching into the president's office, and I remember sitting down and we just come right out and say it: "We need a helicopter."

I remember him saying, "I don't understand."

I tell him, "You've got to know people that have one! Lee Iacocca, Roger Penske—these are huge alumni of the university. These people probably have helicopters, or at least know someone who has a helicopter!" I kept pushing, telling him, "I need an answer in twenty-four hours, because I promised Katie Couric I'd call back and give her an answer."

I remember him saying, "You guys are a trip!" and kicked us out of his office. Later he called me and said, "Okay, Erik, I got you a helicopter." He came through.

I called Katie Couric, told her I had solved the problem. We could pick her up in Connecticut, fly her to Pennsylvania, land her on the soccer field next to the stadium where the graduation would take place, wait for her to speak, and then fly her back home the same evening. How could she say no? She couldn't. In the end, she came, she spoke, she was fabulous!

Now that's a scrappy story! I think the reason that this progression continued was because Erik and his friends didn't "scare the bunny." They were steady, consistent, and classy, but not annoying or off-putting, and their persistence was respectfully appreciated by another scrappy-minded individual. Sometimes a successful scrappy effort depends more on your ability to find workarounds. Being focused on a goal is important, even essential, but so is being nimble enough to adjust to setbacks without giving up altogether.

Moral of the story: Even with the best of intentions, your strategy might have to morph and shift in ways that you hadn't anticipated, but if you maintain your scrappy attitude and stay the course, things can work out exactly as you hoped.

In these three stories, we see the long, winding, and sometimes frustrating journey a scrappy effort can take before it comes to fruition. An inspired idea in and of itself is not nearly enough. It must be reinforced with dedication and the willingness to show up and be fueled by a desire to rise above the field and shine in a unique way.

I hope you noticed the specific scrappy moments in each of these stories where the individual seriously had to think creatively, be persistent, and roll up their shirtsleeves and get to work. For Damion it was on the third or fourth attempt when the CEO of Quiksilver threw away his designs and sent him back to the drawing board. He could have quit, but he didn't. He said, "That's it. I'm all in." The CEO never said it, but that's what he was looking for.

For Steven, it was the moment when he was sitting at his computer, ready to send off his beautiful résumé via the Internet like everyone else, and he stopped himself. He said, "Wait a minute. If I send this normal résumé through the normal channels, I'm going to get screened out. I gotta go big." Then he stepped away from the keyboard and rethought his strategy.

Erik Sherman's scrappy moment came when the president of the university said, "You tried, but this isn't going to work. You need to set your sights on another speaker," and Erik responded, "No way!"

A scrappy effort also must be molded by the hands of an individual who is not afraid to change course or double back or go looking for help in unexpected places.

So give it a run. See what happens and let us know. Send us your story so we can share your experience with others. We want to help you celebrate your wins, work through your challenges, and learn with you and from you.

FUTURE CAST (*YES! YOU'VE GOT THIS!*)

This whole book is about those pivotal moments when you have decided that you are going to play big and do something that changes the game. Whether it's just an experiment for your own growth and personal development or a bold act of conviction to move toward a specific goal, you are taking action with hopeful intent.

The only caveat: Don't push beyond a place from which you can reasonably recover. It's okay to put yourself out there, but not at the risk of everything. My advice: risk what you can tolerate losing but no more.

Now it's your turn—you've got this! Pause and consider all that you've done to reach this moment. Try envisioning what the future might look like when your particular scrappy effort—whatever its size, intensity, or risk—succeeds. Imagine how that success might ripple throughout the rest of your career or life.

Now imagine what the future looks like if you do nothing at all . . . boring.

CELEBRATE YOUR SUCCESS

The more you praise and celebrate your life, the more there is in life to celebrate.

—**Oprah Winfrey**

How do you know if your scrappy effort was successful? There's positive movement—cause to celebrate. It either moves your intention forward or you come closer to achieving your goal. You will know it worked because you *feel* the win, big or small.

I'm a huge believer in champagne moments (or celebratory beer, ice cream, night on the town, whatever your preference). You have to celebrate! This journey is supposed to be fun. Stop and take the time to recognize and enjoy the big wins, little wins, and everything in between. Research shows there is bonus value to celebrating.

In her article "Getting Results Through Others," Loraine Kasprzak writes, quoting her coauthor Jean Oursler, "When others have worked hard to achieve the desired results, celebrate it! 'It's important to celebrate because our brains need a memorable reference point—also called a reward—to make the whole journey worthwhile.'"

Celebrating creates a positive benchmark in your brain for future reference. According to an article in the *Journal of Staff Development* by Richard DuFour:

> *Ritual and ceremony help us experience the unseen webs of significance that tie a community together. There may be grand ceremonies for special occasions, but organizations [and individuals] also need simple rituals that infuse meaning and purpose into daily routine. Without ritual and ceremony, transitions become incomplete, a clutter of comings and goings. Life becomes an endless set of Wednesdays.*

An endless set of Wednesdays? Yuck. Who needs that? Whether you are an individual, a small team, or a large organization, celebrate your scrappy wins as part of the experience and enjoy the ride.

THE PURSUIT OF SCRAPPINESS (SCRAPPY = HAPPY)

Harvard University professor Shawn Achor, the author of two books on happiness, has a beautiful definition of happiness that directly relates to the value of being scrappy: "Happiness (noun) is the joy you feel when striving towards your potential."

I believe most of us want to feel empowered and in control, charting our own course. We also want relief from anxiety. Getting scrappy moves us closer to that space, and even if the effort ultimately doesn't land the way you intended, it puts control back in your hands. And when a scrappy effort does land, it can create amazing innovations that make life easier, more enjoyable, and less stressful; more fun. There's something to be learned from the people who don't care if things didn't work out exactly as they had hoped but were just thrilled with the ride. Embrace the freedom that comes with just doing your best and letting it go.

You *decide to go*, and you are standing at the helm. You're not surrendering to chance or luck or another person. I know it's not easy. Getting scrappy takes guts and resolve and a lot of hard work. But take a moment and think of the stories we've explored in this book. At some point in their journey, each of those scrappy individuals was right where you are at this very moment. They were excited, hopeful, frustrated, scared, unsure, curious, fed up, impatient, exhausted, and determined. Yet they didn't stop.

I imagine all of the people in this book, at the outset of their journey, listened to that small voice somewhere deep inside their soul that said, "Yes, I am in, and I'm putting my tush on the line!" Maybe they didn't articulate it in precisely that way, but their behavior to follow certainly illustrated the spirit of that declaration. They forged ahead with scrappy attitudes that morphed into scrappy strategies and eventually amazing wins. That's the magic of getting scrappy. It's incentive and daring and creativity all mixed together into remarkable strategies.

And when it's over, a scrappy effort can even be redemptive. If you have failed in the past, felt the pain of missing the mark, launching a successful scrappy effort can be a liberating experience that you carry with you for the rest of your life. Think about it—who doesn't love a scrappy story?

Remember, you are the main character of your own life story, and when you get scrappy, it makes for fun and interesting chapters. Now is the time for your next chapter. Go forward with hope and get scrappy.

The End.

Or maybe this is just the beginning. . . .

REVIEW

- The final element of getting scrappy is execution.
- Consider the Scrappy Strategy Action Plan Checklist before executing.

- Executing a scrappy effort can unfold in countless ways, reflecting an individual's personality, skills, and dreams of the future.
- Try envisioning what the future might look like if your particular scrappy effort—whatever its size, intensity, or risk—succeeds. Imagine how that success might ripple throughout the rest of your career or life.

Chapter Activity: Review the following checklist and begin to draft your next scrappy strategy.

SCRAPPY STRATEGY ACTION PLAN CHECKLIST

❑ Make the decision to play big and commit—decide to go!

❑ Set your goal.

❑ Identify the recipient: Whom do you need to influence to get where you want to go?

❑ Determine the best time to execute and invest in doing your research and homework.

❑ Start brainstorming and assemble your support team.

❑ Develop your plan: a Plan A and a Plan B.

❑ Conduct a premortem.

❑ Take action.

ACKNOWLEDGMENTS

The cool part about the acknowledgments page is that it's the author's chance to formally thank the people who have supported the writing of her book. This segment of the book is important to me because this work is the combined effort of people who have come together in many different ways. No one accomplishes a goal like writing, releasing, and selling a book without the help of numerous people.

With sincere gratitude, I would like to thank my team, family, friends, and colleagues who have helped bring this project into form.

Thanks to the team at Portfolio/Penguin, specifically Adrian Zackheim, president and publisher, and Bria Sandford, my editor, for their creativity and insight in helping to take this work to another level.

From the day we met, Margret McBride, my literary agent, has believed in me and my vision of this project. Big hugs to you, Margret! And to her right hand, Faye Atchison.

ACKNOWLEDGMENTS

My administrative marketing assistant Katelyn Lucas has been an integral part of organizing, managing, and working with me to edit this content. In addition, she holds down the fort at the office, so I am able to move forward with my speaking engagements and consulting work on the road knowing everything is taken care of back home. Your loyalty and support over this last year have been a huge part of this book's success.

My personal editor, Kari Barlow, has been incredibly helpful in bringing this book to life. She has worked with me over the years to take my speeches, lectures, and seminar writing style and convert it into this manuscript.

I want to thank all of my mentors and coaches for their guidance and support. You were generous enough to share with me your pearls of wisdom to help me navigate the hills and valleys of my journey. A special thank-you goes out to Harvey Mackay. Your guidance and suggestions, even when they were painful, have been invaluable to me.

My critical review team took the time to read the early drafts and provide wonderful feedback and editing suggestions, including Jerry Anderson, Beck Bamberger, Tom Bardenett, Erin Casey, Jim Corboy, Trae Sterling, and Chris Widener. Each of you has helped me make this book a valuable tool for readers.

I would also like to express my deep appreciation to the many corporations, associations, and individuals who have included my programs in their training and development agendas.

A big thank-you to my dear friend (and next-door neighbor when we were teenagers) Mitt Seely for his artwork and creative illustrations in this book.

It was a treat to work with my friends on the back cover photo shoot for this project. Big hugs to my stylist/photography team: Allie Marion (photographer), Natalie Kinsman (hair), Courtney Noelle Maddox (stylist).

A very special thank-you to Mark Fortier with Fortier Public Relations for his commitment to this project before, during, and after the launch.

This project would be nothing without the interviews and shared experiences of the individuals who contributed to *Scrappy.* Thank you all for sharing your brilliant "scrappy success stories."

A very special thank-you goes out to my colleagues and friends at The MacKay Roundtable, National Speakers Association, and Gen Next.

My parents, Jan and Pete Sjodin, my sister Kim, and my extended family members were all part of the manuscript review team or helped promote the book at one time or another. I love you guys.

My dearest friends, old and new, are all such a wonderful gift. On this particular project, I want to give a shout-out to a few guys in my crew as well (as I already acknowledged all the girls in the tree on the dedication page): Ken Deane, Nick Taylor, Rich Thau, and Brad McMillen for their time and consistent willingness to let me share the bits and pieces along the way and for their opinions and contributions.

November 15, 2015, marked Sjodin Communications' twenty-fifth anniversary! I am blown away at how quickly the years have passed. I am honored and humbled to have built this little company and to make a living doing what I love to do.

Thank you all for being part of my journey.

BIBLIOGRAPHY

Acuff, Jon. *Do Over*. New York: Penguin Group, 2015.

Ali, Laila, and David Ritz. *Reach!: Finding Strength, Spirit, and Personal Power*. New York: Hyperion, 2002.

Apollo 13. DVD. Directed by Ron Howard. Produced by Brian Grazer. Universal City Studios, Inc., 1995.

Atkinson, Nancy. "13 Things That Saved Apollo 13, Part 10: Duct Tape." *Universe Today*. N.p., Apr. 26, 2010. www.universetoday.com/63673/13-things -that-saved-apollo-13-part-10-duct-tape/ (accessed Oct. 8, 2015).

Baird, B., J. Smallwood, M. D. Mrazek, J. W. Y. Kam, M. S. Franklin, and J. W. Schooler. "Inspired by Distraction: Mind Wandering Facilitates Creative Incubation." *Psychological Science* 23.10 (2012): 1117–22. www.centenary.edu/attachments/psychology/journal/archive/ 2013septjournalclub.pdf.

Bamberger, Beck. "Uncomfortable Experiences." E-mail interview, December 1, 2015.

Bardenett, Thomas. "Scrappy 1000+ (Scale Your Effort Within an Organization)." Telephone interview, May 5, 2015.

———. "Scrappy 1000+ (Scale Your Effort Within an Organization)— Part 2." Telephone interview, August 17, 2015.

Bello, Marisol. "Pilot: Campaign Reform More Critical Than Security Breach." *USA Today.* N.p., Apr. 19, 2015. www.usatoday.com%2Fstory%2Fnews%2F2015%2F04%2F19%2Fgyrocopter-pilot-interview%2F26028441%2F.

Bernstein, Ross. "Goldie the Gopher." Telephone interview. May 4, 2015.

Beyond the Tank. "Pilot." ABC. May 1, 2015. http://abc.go.com/shows/beyond-the-tank/video/most-recent/VDKA0_705866kt

Capretto, Lisa. "Happiness Researcher Dispels a Big Myth About Joy." *HuffPost OWN.* Dec. 2015. www.huffingtonpost.com/entry/big-myth-about-joy_us_56743dd9e4b0b958f65667d4.

———. "Paulo Coelho Explains How 'The Alchemist' Went from Flop to Record-Breaking Bestseller." *The Huffington Post.* Sept. 4, 2014. Web. www.huffingtonpost.com/2014/09/04/the-alchemist-paulo-coelho-oprah_n_5762092.html.

Cargill, JD. "Orchid CNN." E-mail interview, March 23, 2015.

Carreau, Debby. "Milestones Restaurant—X Factor." Telephone interview, November 11, 2015.

Cohen, Jared. "Elements of Getting Scrappy." Personal interview, June 2015.

Deutsch, Donny, and Peter Knobler. *Often Wrong, Never in Doubt: Unleash the Business Rebel Within.* New York: Harper Business, 2005.

DiEdwardo, Judy Alexandra. "Making It Big." *Success.* Nov. 3, 2008. www.success.com/article/making-it-big (accessed Apr. 1, 2015).

DuFour, Richard. "Why Celebrate?" *Journal of Staff Development* 19.4 (1998): 58.

Dugan, Regina. From Mach-20 Glider to Hummingbird Drone." TED. Mar. 2012. www.ted.com/talks/regina_dugan_from_march_20_glider_to_humming_bird_drone (accessed June 2015).

———, and Kaigham Gabriel. "'Special Forces' Innovation: How DARPA Attacks Problems." *Harvard Business Review.* Oct. 1, 2013. https://hbr.org/2013/10/special-forces-innovation-how-darpa-attacks-problems/ar/1.

Dunbar, Brian. "Apollo 13." NASA. July 8, 2009. www.nasa.gov/mission_pages/apollo/missions/apollo13.html.

Eadicicco, Lisa. "A Woman Created an Awesome Resume to Land Her Dream Job at Airbnb—and It Caught the CEO's Attention Immediately."

Business Insider. Apr. 22, 2015. www.businessinsider.com/nina-mufleh -airbnb-resume-2015-4 (accessed May 14, 2015).

Fink, Ken. "Leave Room for Serendipity." Telephone interview, May 7, 2015.

Freiman, Roy. "The Nature of Being Scrappy." Personal interview, June 2015.

Gage, Randy. "Adult Diaper Mailer." Telephone interview, September 11, 2015.

Gilbert, Elizabeth. *Big Magic: Creative Living Beyond Fear.* New York: Riverhead, 2015.

Grazer, Brian, and Charles Fishman. *A Curious Mind: The Secret to a Bigger Life.* New York: Simon & Schuster, 2015.

"Gyrocopter Pilot's New Campaign: Push Congress to Sign No-Lobbying Pledge." *Washington Post.* Aug. 27, 2015.

Hague, Greg. "How to Learn Twice as Much in Half the Time." E-mail interview, May 2, 2015.

Harris, Jenn. "Girl Scout Sells Cookies Outside Pot Dispensary: 117 Boxes in 2 Hours." *Los Angeles Times.* Feb. 21, 2014. www.latimes.com/food/ dailydish/la-dd-girl-scout-sells-cookies-pot-clinic-20140221-story .html (accessed Apr. 1, 2015).

Hassler, Christine. "Are You Willing to Work for Free in Hopes of Gaining an Opportunity?" Telephone interview, May 20, 2015.

Hickman, Damion. "Quiksilver T-shirt Designs." Telephone interview, September 23, 2015.

Horowitz, Ben. *The Hard Thing About Hard Things.* New York: Harper-Collins, 2014.

"Is a Gyrocopter Landing on Capitol Lawn a Threat?" *USA Today.* Apr. 21, 2015: 6A.

Jeff. "Inside This Box Is One Amazing Résumé (17 HQ Photos)." *TheCHIVE RSS.* Aug. 24, 2015. http://thechive.com/2015/08/24/inside-this-box-is-one-amazing-resume-17-hq-photos/ (accessed Aug. 25, 2015).

Kasprzak, Loraine. "Getting Results Through Others." *Chemical Engineering Progress* 111.8 (2015): 19.

Kaufman, Josh. "The First 20 Hours: How to Learn Anything . . . Fast." E-mail interview, October 28, 2015.

Kelly, Ryan. "Dollar Tulip Trade Show Booth." E-mail interview, March 26, 2015.

Klein, Gary. "Performing a Project Premortem." *Harvard Business Review*. N.p., Sept. 1, 2007. https://hbr.org/2007/09/performing-a-project-premortem/ar/1 (accessed 2015).

Ko, Toni. "Know When to Back Off." Telephone interview. Mar. 14, 2015.

Lacy, Nick. "On Execution." Telephone interview, September 30, 2015.

Lee, Brian. "The Artist's Dilemma." *Genius Types*. N.p., Mar. 6, 2007. http://geniustypes.com/the_artists_dilemma/ (accessed Sept. 22, 2015).

"Making Change Decisions." *Revolutionizing Higher Education in Agriculture* (n.d.): 71–87. IBM Corporation, Oct. 2008. www-07.ibm.com/au/pdf/making_change_work.pdf (accessed June 2015).

McMillen, Brad. "Sea of Sameness." E-mail interview, Feb. 21, 2015.

Melish, Stephanie. "Keep the Long Game in Mind." E-mail interview, January 27, 2016.

Nisen, Max. "Here's What 'Shark Tank' Looks Like in 9 Different Countries." *Business Insider*. Nov. 12, 2013. www.businessinsider.com/shark-tank-international-versions-2013-11#ixzz3l0TqPWqf (accessed Sept. 6, 2015).

"Our Heritage." *Selfridges*. Selfridges&Co, n.d. www.selfridges.com/US/en/content/our-heritage (accessed Aug. 28, 2015).

Palmer, Brian. "Dustbuster, Pizza to Nurses." Telephone interview, April 28, 2015.

Peck, Emily. "Why Walking Meetings Can Be Better Than Sitting Meetings." *The Huffington Post*. Apr. 9, 2015. www.huffingtonpost.com/2015/04/09/walking-meetings-at-linke_n_7035258.html (accessed June 1, 2015).

Petrone, Paul. "The Brilliant Airbnb Job Application Stunt (That Actually Worked)." *LinkedIn Talent Blog*. Apr. 24, 2015. http://talent.linked in.com/blog/index.php/2015/04/the-brilliant-airbnb-job-application-stunt-that-actually-worked (accessed May 14, 2015).

Richter, Sam. "The 3x5 Rule/Watercolor Painting, Build a Customized Personal Web Site." Telephone interview, May 4, 2015.

Riker, Jennifer Matthey. "Getting Scrappy to Move Your Personal Goals Forward." E-mail interview, December 17, 2015.

Robinson, Ken, Ph.D., and Lou Aronica. *The Element*. New York: Penguin Group, 2009.

Schussler, Steven. "Rainforest Café, Crashed Meeting." Telephone interview, May 19, 2015.

————, and Marvin Karlins. *It's a Jungle in There*. New York: Sterling Publishing, 2010.

Shapiro, Stephen. "7 Ways to Outsmart Your Brain to Be More Innovative." American Express. Nov. 14, 2012. www.americanexpress.com/us/small-business/openforum/articles/7-ways-to-outsmart-your-brains-wiring-and-become-more-innovative/.

Sherman, Erik. "Katie Couric Graduation Speaker." Telephone interview. May 1, 2015.

"Shipping Flour by Mail Called 'Inappropriate.'" *Seattle Post-Intelligencer*. Nov. 6, 2001: n.p.

Sjodin, Terri L. *Small Message, Big Impact: The Elevator Speech Effect*. New York: Portfolio, 2012.

Sly, Susan. "Get Scrappy to Turn Things Around." Telephone interview. October 21, 2015.

Stainton, Bill. "The Shower Is Your Personal Idea Booth" E-mail interview. September 15, 2015.

Steiner, Brandon. "Selling a Little Dirt." Telephone interview. May 5, 2015.

————. *You Gotta Have Balls*. Hoboken, N.J.: John Wiley & Sons, 2012. 139–42.

Sweeney, Joe. "Bob Costas and a Case of Brats." Telephone interview, May 11, 2015.

Taube, John. "Scrappy." *Urban Dictionary*. Dec. 9, 2004. Web. www.urbandictionary.com/define.php?term=scrappy accessed Jan. 1, 2015.

Tsunder, Roman. "Dalai Lama." E-mail interview, April 26, 2015.

"Union Slams Flour Company Mail Campaign." *The Tuscaloosa News*. Nov. 7, 2001. Web. https://news.google.com/newspapers?nid=1817&dat=20011107&id=wUogAAAAIBAJ&sjid=DKYEAAAAIBAJ&pg=4413%2C1251057&hl=en (accessed Sept. 11, 2015).

Wall Street. DVD. Directed by Oliver Stone. Twentieth Century Fox Film Corporation, 1987.

Walther, George. "The Wooden Spoon." E-mail interview, August 15, 2015.

Weber, Jeff, and Jeff Cova. "Winspire." E-mail and telephone interviews, January 20, 2016.

Wickman, Floyd, and Terri Sjodin. *Mentoring: The Most Obvious Yet Overlooked Key to Achieving More in Life Than You Dreamed Possible: A Success Guide for Mentors and Protégés*. Boston: McGraw-Hill, 1997.

Varela, Steven. "Wizards of the Coast Résumé." Telephone interview, September 23, 2015.

———. "Wizards of the Coast Résumé." *Imgur*. N.p., Aug. 2015. Web. http://imgur.com/a/8QJsx (accessed Sept. 2015).

Young, Zeynep. "When Playing Small Is a Risky Play." Telephone interview, November 17, 2015.

INDEX